E$TATE $ALE RICHE$

E$TATE $ALE RICHE$

✦

A Manual for Making Money at Estate Sales

M. D. Baker
and
Abigail L. Baker

iUniverse, Inc.

New York Lincoln Shanghai

E$TATE $ALE RICHE$
A Manual for Making Money at Estate Sales

Copyright © 2006 by M. D. Baker

iUniverse books may be ordered through booksellers or by contacting:

iUniverse
2021 Pine Lake Road, Suite 100
Lincoln, NE 68512
www.iuniverse.com
1-800-Authors (1-800-288-4677)

ISBN-13: 978-0-595-39300-8 (pbk)
ISBN-13: 978-0-595-83693-2 (ebk)
ISBN-10: 0-595-39300-4 (pbk)
ISBN-10: 0-595-83693-3 (ebk)

Printed in the United States of America

Contents

Introduction

What is an estate sale?

An estate sale is a sale of a person's personal possessions, normally held to settle the estate after the person has died. The sale typically takes place in the person's home and includes the entire contents of the house.

Why are estate sales so profitable?

There are two basic reasons why estate sales are so profitable. First, the contents of many homes contain a large number of items that have been collected or accumulated over a long period of time. Sometimes objects are over a hundred years old. Many estate sales contain large quantities of antiques and other valuable older items.

The second reason that estate sales are so profitable is that most items are priced well below their actual value. Most individuals are unaware of the true value of the items they are selling, and in order to settle the estate, families are anxious to sell or get rid of the items as quickly as possible. Normally estate sales last for only two days.

Estate sales offer an excellent opportunity to make large profits by buying a large number of under priced antiques and other valuable items.

Who is this book for?

This book is for anyone interested in the thrill and excitement of making money searching for and discovering valuable objects. Like hunting the hulls of sunken treasure ships, estate sales are nothing less than treasure hunts for valuable objects in the attics, basements, and other rooms of old houses. And there is plenty of treasure to be found in these old houses: jewelry, coins, valuable glass, furniture, pottery…the list of treasures is endless. And at any estate sale, there is always the possibility that you will find a truly valuable item—a lost treasure—and become instantly wealthier.

This book will help individuals who are already familiar with estate sales increase their profits, but it is primarily meant to show individuals who are unfamiliar with estate sales how profitable and exciting an estate sale can actually be.

It is also for the newcomer who would like to find a profitable and rewarding hobby or small business.

Why I wrote this book

I have written this book to show readers how it is possible to make tens of thousands of dollars at estate sales. I have been going to estate sales for over twenty years and have found that there are many shortcuts, tricks, and strategies that can make estate sales much more profitable. The main objective of any estate sale is to find and buy the largest quantity of valuable items that you can. In this book, I will show you how this can be accomplished by following a few simple guidelines. I will also discuss how and where to sell the items you purchase at estate sales for the greatest return on your money.

I hope this book will show you how fun, exciting, and profitable estate sales can be. Attend one, following the information in this book, and you will see what I am talking about. You will make money and have fun doing it!

1

Having Fun Making Money

It is seven o'clock in the morning, and the line of people standing in front of the house waiting for the estate sale to begin continues to grow longer. There are, in my estimation, already about forty people in line, even though the sale is not scheduled to start for another hour. The line of people winds across the porch, down the steps, and halfway down the block. Cars move slowly up and down the narrow street in front of the house, stopping and letting people out to join the line. I have been standing in the line now for just over thirty minutes. It's bitterly cold and windy. The snow crunches under my numb feet as I rock back and forth, trying to stay warm.

I imagine my wife, sitting in the warm car at the end of the block, maybe giving me a disgusted look for dragging her out so early to yet another estate sale. But the car is parked too far down the street to really tell what she's doing. I convinced her to come with me to the estate sale by showing her the ad for the sale. The ad stated that there was going to be "much antique jewelry" for sale. My wife is an avid collector of vintage jewelry and is somewhat of a self-taught expert in the field. She knows how to judge quality and age and can recognize most of the maker's marks, and she has made many excellent buys at past estate sales; however, she refuses to wait in the cold.

I am excited about this sale and what valuable items I might find inside the house. I think about the person who recently found a valuable map at an estate sale not far away from the site of this sale. He found the map at the bottom of an old box of papers. He paid $25 for the whole box, and at the time, he thought he had probably paid too much. But the map ended up being worth over $200,000. I was not at that estate sale, but I very easily could have been.

Could there be something that valuable at this estate sale? It happens frequently. Valuable items are found and bought for a few dollars, but are worth hundreds or even thousands of dollars. I have done it myself many times. Three months ago, I bought an item at an estate sale for $5 and sold it for $1,100.

The ad for the estate sale read: "100-year-old estate, entire contents to be sold, house packed from attic to basement, antiques, toys, much antique jewelry, furniture, vintage clothing from the turn of the century, some old coins, old radios, just too much to list." Looking up at the old Victorian three-story brick house, I believe the ad was likely accurate. If the house holds even half the valuable antiques that were listed in the ad, then it will likely be a very profitable sale.

The rumor floating around at the sale is that the owner was ninety years old when she died five years earlier and had lived in the house her whole life.

I watch as a woman comes from around the side of the house. She shields her eyes as she looks into a basement window. I have already been around the house and peered through all the windows I could see into, attempting to take an inventory of items that will be sold, but the trip didn't give me any real clues as to which room of the house holds the most valuable items or where I should start my search. At some estate sales, you can locate valuable items before the sale even begins by looking through the windows; then you can go directly to that room when the sale starts. I think there might be a McCoy vase in one of the bedrooms, but I am not certain enough to go directly to that room. I will probably take another trip around the house now that it's brighter, but I'm concerned that if I do, I might lose my place in line. At estate sales, it's important to keep your place in line so that you can be one of the first buyers inside the house.

Looking through the windows, I did notice a lot of collectible glass. My wife will be happy; she collects glass and knows a lot about most glass items. I'm convinced, however, that she has waited much too long to get out of the car and into the line and everything valuable will likely be gone by the time she gets inside the house. *Maybe she's in line,* I tell myself. I can't see the dome light on inside the car anymore, but I can't see her standing in line either.

The crowd continues to grow. Even though I have a good view down the street, I can no longer see the end of the line. There must be well over a hundred people standing in line now.

The wait seems endless. The closer it gets to eight o'clock, the more nervous I become. By now, everyone has become excited and impatient. I have been waiting for over an hour and a half, but it seems like much longer by the time one of the sellers inside the house opens the front door and lets us in. We all march quickly up the steps, across the porch, and into the house.

Once inside the house, I am not disappointed. The ad was accurate. The house is truly packed with antique items. It looks like a house that has been undisturbed since the 1950s. A motion lamp sits idle on a coffee table, but it is gone by the time I get there. I grab for and am lucky to get a small box full of advertising items sitting on a table. In one of the bedrooms, I find a stack of old games. In the corner, I notice some old tin toys. There are people frantically looking at the items on the tables, but they have all failed to notice the toys just beneath them. I move as quickly as possible across the room and take all the toys from the box. In the basement, I find two old store displays, still in their original wrapping, and a lighted sign advertising Otto Milk that's most likely from the fifties. I also find a box full of advertising items from Kentucky Fried Chicken: a pin, some old menus, and an award plaque. I find a small, like-new Philco transistor radio in the garage, along with a bag of marbles. There are items everywhere: on the floor, on tables, under tables, in boxes, and in every corner of the house. I quickly move off toward the living room, picking up items and putting them in my container as I go (a bank, some old pens, and an ashtray), and then quickly move to another room. The movement of the people in the house up to this point has been frantic and chaotic, but I can already sense the crowd beginning to thin.

I spend the better part of the next two hours systematically going over every square inch of the house, carefully examining all the items in every room, looking though drawers and boxes and checking the bottoms of closets. I try not to miss anything. I have learned from previous sales that you are likely to find valuable items just about anywhere in a house.

By the time I have finished my search, I have packed three cardboard boxes full of items that I believe are valuable. I have been dragging the boxes around the rooms and through the crowds like a pack rat the whole time. I've collected advertising items, jewelry, magazines, old toys, books, and much more. I'm certain that one item that's priced at $5 is worth over $100, and there are a number of other items that in my opinion are greatly under priced. After a quick estimate, I am convinced that the items I have gathered, costing me just over $100, will likely bring close to $500 when I resell them.

It has been a good day, I feel. I have had better days, but this day was good, and I'm satisfied with the items that I have found. I have passed my wife a couple of times. Once she reached in her shopping bag and picked out a "Charlie the Tuna" watch and handed it to me. I couldn't believe that I had missed it. She too has ended up with a large shopping bag full of items—a collection of glass items, a number of pieces of jewelry, and some vintage ladies' clothes and accessories. She reluctantly tells me that she is glad that she came.

This is how I have spent most of my Saturday mornings for the last twenty years, traveling around the city to search though old houses for valuable antiques at estate sales. And most mornings, I can hardly wait for the sale to get started. It is one of the most exciting things I have experienced. In my opinion, an estate sale is the closest thing to a treasure hunt that exists today. Many older estates are gold mines filled with hundreds of valuable antiques. Over the years, I have made thousands of dollars buying valuable antiques at estate sales.

What is an estate sale? Although the definition is somewhat nebulous, an estate sale generally means a sale of all of an individual's possessions, the sale normally being held in the owner's home. Estate sales are normally held when the owner of an estate dies; occasionally they are held when a person moves. This means that virtually everything is up for sale—jewelry, clothing, furniture, cars, tools—everything that the individual owned is normally sold. Sometimes an individual has lived in the same house for years and has accumulated thousands of items over a lifetime. Many of these items are very old and very valuable.

For the most part, estate sales are mecca of valuable and antique items, many of which (if not all) are under priced. There are two main reasons that most estate-sale items are under priced. First, most families are unaware of their true value. And in many cases, the main objective of the sale is to settle the estate as quickly as possible, and this means selling the items as quickly as possible, usually during a two-day sale. To sell quickly often requires selling items cheaply, so you can often find fantastic bargains. Valuable items can usually be purchased for literally pennies on the dollar. It is therefore relatively simple to make a significant amount of money at these sales; over the years, I have made thousands of dollars buying valuable estate items for much less than their true value and selling them later for a large profit. Most items at estate sales are priced anywhere from $1 to $50, but most of the time, they are worth much more. It is commonplace to buy items for a tenth the price you will realize when the item is resold. As a matter of fact, this is the rule rather than the exception, and I normally expect to get at least a return of between five and ten times the amount I paid for an item when I resell it. Although I have never found an exceptionally valuable item (one worth $10,000 to $50,000), they do exist and are found almost daily at estate sales.

The main reason for the excitement of an estate sale is the possibility that you may find some truly valuable items and make thousands of dollars. On any given day, you might find an item worth $100,000.

At some estate sales, almost every item being sold is old, and these are the sales that are the most exciting and profitable to attend. These are the sales you need to locate and attend to be truly financially successful.

Even if you are unable to find any truly valuable antiques, you will almost certainly make money on the items that you do find. Often the thrill and excitement of the hunt is reward enough for your efforts. It is also exciting finding that an item you bought is worth even more than you thought it was worth. I have frequently purchased items for a couple dollars, thinking they couldn't be worth anything more than $15 or $20, but later selling them for twenty times that amount.

Over the years, I have started to view estate sales as somewhat of a game: a treasure hunt, the object of which is to buy the greatest number of valuable items and make the most amount of money when they are resold. It is, in essence, a game I believe you can become very good at playing. Like playing a game over and over, you eventually get to the point where you are better than all the other players. The better you understand the rules and regulations and the more you play, the better you will get and the more money you will make. Like every game, there are tricks and strategies that give you advantages that will help you find more valuables and make more money. One of my main reasons for writing this book is to point out these tricks and strategies that I have learned over the years and have found very useful. I think this will give the beginner a basic understanding of the mechanics behind estate sales, but I also believe that these strategies will be beneficial to the seasoned estate-sale shopper. In short, with this book, I hope to describe to you how to make the most amount of money at estate sales by finding and buying the largest number of valuable antiques.

I also believe this book will benefit collectors. Estate sales are an excellent way to add to collections and find reasonably priced items that are often difficult to afford at antique stores or auctions. They also offer an excellent opportunity to expand your hobby by exposing you to many different items. I have become a collector of many items since I have begun to attend estate sales, and I have built some valuable collections at very reasonable prices. This is not only a hobby, but also an investment, since most of the items that you collect will increase in value over time.

You may also decide to start your own small business selling the antiques you have purchased at estate sales. This can be very lucrative and enjoyable, and it can provide a substantial second income. Estate sales can be profitable for everyone, but are particularly suited for the older individual who already possesses a working knowledge of older items.

This book is divided into five sections. The first section describes how to find the best estate sales to attend. The second chapter gives an overview of what items you will most likely encounter and which items you should consider buying at estate sales. The third chapter tells you what you should do on the day of an estate sale and lists other venues where you can buy valuable items, and the fourth section tells you where you can sell your items. Finally, the fifth section provides tips that will be helpful when attending estate sales. I hope you will enjoy reading this book, and I also hope that you will someday experience the fun and excitement of attending an estate sale.

The estate sale that I described at the beginning of this chapter was an actual sale I attended, and I have listed the items I bought, how much I paid for them, and what I sold them for later. It is not absolutely complete. One item turned out to be broken, two smaller items were sold with a group of other estate items, and three other items didn't sell at all, but I lost less than $15 on those items. The sale items below are essentially a true representation of a typical estate sale. Some are not this profitable, but many are more profitable than this sale was. As you can see, my total profit was around $600. Considering the time I spent, I made about a hundred dollars an hour at this sale.

Item	Purchase Price	Sale Price
1. Figural hand-carved bottle stopper	$4.00	$13.75
2. New York World's Fair ashtray	25¢	$4.50
3. M. S. Sobieski advertising pen	25¢	$3.50
4. MIT advertising pen	25¢	$2.00
5. Bag of older marbles	$3.00	$16.75
6. Advertising matchbooks	$2.50	$8.75
(Pepsi, Bit-O-Honey, Dr. West's Toothbrushes)		
7. Two railroad timetables	$1.00	$8.50
8. TWA travel book	25¢	$5.00
9. Girl Scout hanky (Idaho Roundup 1965)	25¢	$16.50
10. Old candy box (1960s TV theme)	$5.00	$47.50
11. Roy Rogers book (1951)	25¢	$6.50
12. Three golf balls (circa 1910)	$1.00	$63.75
13. Kids' games (Park and Ride, Jetsons)	$8.00	$127.00
14. TWA metal pin	25¢	$4.00
15. Red Cross blood donor pin (very old)	25 ¢	$3.00

16. Four Japanese tin cars from the 1960s	$40.00	$179.50
17. Two old schoolbook tablets	$4.00	$8.75
18. Otto Milk lighted advertising sign	$8.00	$40.75
19. KFC items(pin, plaque, menu)	$8.50	$32.50
20. Cracker Jack bank and prize	$4.00	$36.25
21. Coca-Cola menu (1950s)	$2.00	$12.75
22. Two store displays (Halloween)	$15.00	$57.00
23. "Charlie the Tuna" watch	$3.00	$21.50
Total:	**$111.00**	**$719.00**

As you can see, estate sales can be very profitable. Incidentally, my wife also did well that day; she bought three relatively valuable pieces of jewelry, a couple of silk scarves, and a piece of Hull pottery, and stayed warm doing it.

Good luck, and happy hunting!

2

Finding the Best Estate Sale

Getting started

One of the most important factors, for a successful estate-sale experience, is to determine which of the many estate sales you should actually attend. Since on any given Saturday there can be anywhere from twenty-five to thirty-five estate sales in your area, determining the best sales to attend can often be a challenge. It should be noted that all estate sales are not created equal. Some sales are exceptionally good, whereas others are hardly worth attending. In this chapter, I will go through the process I normally use to determine the sales that are likely to be the best or the most profitable. Although the process is not fail-safe, it is a relatively objective way of choosing the estate sales that are likely to hold the most potential and eliminating sales that are likely to be unprofitable. In essence, your first objective is to find the estate sale that contains the most affordable and valuable items. It can be a somewhat tedious experience searching out the best sales, but in the long run, the time you spend doing this will be time well spent. What you absolutely don't want to do is to attend an estate sale where there are very few or no valuable items to buy—and this can happen very easily if you don't do your homework.

Gathering the ads

The first step in the process of finding the best sale is to locate as many estate sales as you can that will be occurring in your area on any given date. I normally start this process toward the middle of the week for sales that are typically held on the weekends. Estate-sale listings can be found through a number of sources. Most notably, estate sales are listed in the classifieds section of the local newspapers under the headings "Estate Sales," "Liquidations," or "Garage Sales." I must emphasize newspapers as a source of listings, since in any particular area there may be three or four different newspapers where estate sales are advertised. In my area, which is north of a larger city, I routinely check the ads in two local papers and two regional newspapers. It is important to check as many sources as possible for estate sales listings; this will increase your chances of finding the best sales and assure that you don't miss any exceptionally good sales in your area. Most of these listings can be checked online through the newspaper's Web site.

Besides newspapers, there are other places where you can find estate-sale listings, such as local trade papers and other Web sites. Most of the sales listed in local trade publications can also be accessed through the trade papers' Web sites. I routinely check two trade publications' online sites each week. There are some trade papers that advertise estate sales that have no Web sites. You can usually find these trade papers at local grocery stores, convenience stores, or gas stations. They are normally free publications, and although they are not a great source of estate sales, they occasional list sales that are worth knowing about. This process of collecting the ads typically leaves me with a list of about twenty-five to thirty-five estate sales.

Once I have collected all the ads from all my sources, I separate them according to which days the sales actually begin. This way I can determine not just the best overall estate sale, but also the best sale for any given day. This is important; although most estate sales begin on Saturday, many begin on Friday, and frequently they begin on other days of the week. I should mention that estate sales that start on days other than Saturday can be very profitable, since many people that work are unable to attend sales that are held during the week. I highly recommend that you attempt to attend these sales whenever possible.

When I am done separating the ads according to which days they begin, I start the process of weeding out the good estate sales from the estate sales I feel are unlikely to be profitable.

One important principle that I believe should be followed is that you should only attempt to attend one estate sale on any given day. The main reason for this principle is that by the time you arrive at a second estate sale, most of the valuable items will have been sold. In general, most valuable items at estate sales are sold within the first twenty to thirty minutes, and at the outside, in the first hour. This is not always the case, but I have found that in general, this principle holds true. The second reason to concentrate on just one sale is that attempting to rush to another estate sale may cause you to miss many valuable items at the first sale. It's important to focus on just one estate sale, and it should be the best estate sale you can locate. However, I should point out that I normally pick out an alternative estate sale—a runner-up in the search for the best sale—for reasons that I will mention later.

Analyzing the ads

Once you have gathered your ads and separated them by day of sale, the next step is to analyze each one of the listings separately. Your ultimate goal is to gather enough information from them to decide which estate sales offer the most promise. Some sales can be eliminated almost immediately by what the ad does or doesn't state, but with some ads, it is difficult to determine just how good the estate sale might turn out to be, especially when all you have to go on is an ad of fifty words or less, and especially if the sellers have purposely attempted to make the sale sound better than it is, just to draw a larger crowd. This is a problem that is often very difficult to avoid. When analyzing the ads, I normally use the following list. I find that when I use this list as a template for determining the best estate sale, I can usually narrow the number of potentially good estate-sale listings down to two or three. The items in the list are not necessarily listed in order of importance. The importance of each item often varies depending on the sale itself.

1. Location and address of the estate sale

2. Items listed to be sold

3. Is the sale being run by a professional, or by the family? Is there a pre-sale?

4. Where did the ad appear?

5. Information concerning the age and size of the estate

6. Is there a phone number listed?

7. Distance you have to travel to the estate sale

8. What time and day of the week does the sale begin?

1. Location and address of the estate sale

When attempting to find the best sale, one of the most important factors to take into consideration is that of the actual location of the sale. You can determine much from this single factor. Old houses have a greater potential for being older estates with a better likelihood of containing older, valuable items. Newer homes present just the opposite situation. These estates will usually contain mostly newer items and very few items that are actually old. Ideally, you want to find an estate sale where the residents have lived at the address for at least forty years, and preferably longer. Old addresses in old neighborhoods normally fit this description. The lower the street number, the better; typically, the nearer the house is to the downtown area, the better the sale will be. This is not a blanket validation of all older address, though, since many older homes have changed hands many times. Estate sales with rural addresses also have the potential to be good sales.

If you are unsure of the location of the sale from the address given, then it is best to find it on a map or look up the address online to determine the general location of the sale. Is it in an older section of town, or is it in a newer housing development? Normally you don't want to attend a sale in a house that is less than thirty years old. Many of these houses are located in housing plans or developments. Most new plans are evident from just looking at the street layout on maps, or they can be inferred from the newer-sounding addresses that include such words as "court," "estate," or "acres." A newer-sounding street address leads one to believe that it is a relatively new house and unlikely to contain many older valuable items. If the address is four digits or more, it's also less likely to be an older address. This is not to say that there are not good estate sales at newer houses or apartments, but most of these sales do not contain the older items that tend to be under priced.

Many people do attend sales at houses with newer items, especially in affluent neighborhoods. There are normally many valuable items at these sales, often including many antiques, but as a general rule, most of the items are overpriced or priced just below retail; in my experience, it is much more difficult to make a large profit at these estate sales. I will attend estate sales at newer houses if there are extenuating circumstances. For example, if I know the owner is a retired Coca-Cola employee, then I will likely attend the sale in the hope that there will be a significant amount of Coca-Cola ephemera. I also eliminate most estate sales that are being held strictly because the family is moving, regardless of the address. Families tend to take most of their valuable items with them when they change residency. I almost never attend any estate sales that are being held at apartments or condominiums. These estates are usually not old, and they very seldom contain any significant amount of older and more valuable items. I almost always attend estate sales that involve businesses that have gone out of business or are going out of business. These estate sales often contain a lot of collectible items, especially advertising items. It is also very helpful to know how long the family has resided at the address. It is actually one of the most important factors, but it is also something that is not always easy to determine. In some areas, you can check county real-estate sales records to determine when the house was last sold. If the house has been sold recently, then it is a sale that I will likely eliminate from my list.

Once you have decided that the house listed in the address is an older house, you can add it to your list of potential estate sales to attend. If it's a newer house in a newer section of the city or in a housing plan, I normally eliminate it from further consideration. I also normally eliminate any estate sales being held in apartments, or condominiums, and any estate sales held because the family is moving.

2. Items listed to be sold

Next, look at each ad for the lists of items that are being sold. There are positive items, and there are negative items. You must look at every item listed individually. The fact that they list a wringer-washer, for example, tells you more about what they don't have than what they do have. If this is one of the best items, and sellers usually try to list some of their better items, then it is a sale that probably will not be all that profitable to attend, and I usually eliminate it from my list. It may also indicate that most of the valuable items have been taken by family members or by dealers. On the other hand, if the ad states that there are many antiques, or lists certain categories of collectibles or antiques (such as glassware), or lists specific items that are of value (such as Roseville or some other famous maker), then the sale has the potential to be profitable. If the ad states that there is children's clothing or lists a lot of newer items, especially toys, then I tend to eliminate that sale from my list. As I mentioned earlier, newer items are less likely to bring the large profits that older collectible items can command. Any mention of children's items normally means that the family is younger, and the estate is unlikely to contain many older, valuable items. If I get the sense that the items listed are from a newer estate or that there are unlikely to be any older, valuable items, then I eliminate the ad from my list.

3. Is the sale being run by a professional, or by the family? Is there a pre-sale?

Next, determine who is actually running the estate sale: is it the family, or is it a professional organization? This is a very important factor in determining the best sale. Estate sales conducted by professionals can be problematic at times, and in general, it is better to attend estate sales run by family members. Families are less likely to overprice their items and typically know less about the true value of most items. Most of the time, the families' main concern is just to sell as much merchandise as they can as quickly as possible, since most of the time they have only two or three days to sell the entire contents of the house. They also don't typically have other tangible venues where they can sell their items, which makes them more willing to take less money for an item.

Professionals, on the other hand, have other outlets for the items they might not be able to sell at their estate sales, so they are less likely to price an item cheaply (or at times, even reasonably), and they are less likely to reduce their original prices significantly. Most of the time, they work with dealers who will price items for them, and usually the prices are too high to make any significant profit when you attempt to resell the item. Many dealers will also buy items at the end of the sale for less than they have priced them for the sale. Dealers tell the professionals what they think the value of the items are; of course, it's just their opinion, and they can be wrong; but most of the time, they would not pay those prices, and often they couldn't even sell them at their shops for those prices. Professionals also tend to have pre-sales, which are sales of estate items to dealers and other buyers before the actual estate sale starts; when this happens, most of the valuable antiques have been sold or picked over before the actual estate sale begins. It should also be noted that often professionals will salt their sales with their own items or with items they couldn't sell at other estate sales, especially jewelry. I cannot remember the last time I went to an estate sale run by professionals that didn't have a display case full of jewelry that the professionals brought with them to the sale. Many times they are trying to pass off newer items as vintage. This practice can make it difficult to determine which items are actually old and valuable and which items are reproductions. It can also legitimize cheap reproductions by selling them with authentic antiques. This is a form of deception that can cost you hundreds of dollars if you are not careful. It is also discouraging to find an item that you know has been salted into the sale, because if you find one salted item, you can never be sure that there are not more—and usually there are. After a while, you can usually determine which professionals run acceptable estate sales and which do not. I tend to stay away from sales by professionals who have demonstrated bad practices in the past.

Some professionals run excellent sales where there has been no salting, and the prices are realistic. Over the years, though trial and error, I have been able to determine which professional sales are worth attending. And at times, professionals can be very helpful. You can usually contact them before the sale begins and get information about what items are going to be sold, and if they know what items you are interested in buying, they will often contact you when they have these items to sell. I usually eliminate professionally run sales where I know that the prices are likely to be high and that the items are likely to have been picked over before the sale. I do, however, occasionally put these sales on as an alternate site. I have found many times that the items are so overpriced that they go unsold and can be purchased later, when the prices are reduced. Usually, prices at estate sales are cut drastically in the afternoon of a one-day sale or the second day of a two-day sale. I have made many excellent buys using this strategy.

Many professional estate-sale managers have pre-sales. Normally, a professional running a sale keeps a list of prospective buyers (often many dealers) that she contacts before the actual sale, to inform them of a time they can come to view and buy items from the estate. This sale usually occurs a couple of days before the actual estate sale. It's very important—and I cannot emphasis this enough—to do everything you can to get your name on as many lists for pre-sales as you can. You can often find some excellent buys at these pre-sales, and it is also another means of eliminating an estate sale from your list. If you can attend the pre-sale, then you do not have to worry about attending the actual estate sale later.

It should also be noted that it might actually be good to attend sales run by professionals, since professionals generally will not manage an estate sale unless they believe that the estate has value enough for them to make a significant profit. Therefore, it can be assumed that most professionally run estate sales are estates that have significant value. This should be taken into account when attempting to determine the best estate sales. I also call the professional services that run estate sales every couple of weeks to find out about any upcoming sales they may have scheduled, so that I am sure not to miss any sales or pre-sales.

4. Where did the ad appear?

This is not a major consideration, but at times, it can be important. If the listing appeared in one or two of the larger newspapers in the area, then there will likely be a large number of buyers at the sale, and competition for the valuable items will be greater. It also might mean the sellers feel it is a large enough sale to advertise more widely; thus, there could be an abundance of valuable items at the sale. If, however, the sale appears only in one of the smaller trade papers, then the crowd of buyers will likely be significantly smaller. I will occasionally attend a sale for just this very reason. I have been to many poorly advertised sales where I have had the pick of the items being sold. Unfortunately, most of the sales that are only advertised in small trade papers are estate sales that tend to have less overall value. Ideally, at any estate sale, you want as little competition as possible. The more places the ad appears, the more likely it is that the competition will be greater. I normally don't eliminate any sale from my list of potentially good sales strictly based on where the ad appeared, but I place the ads for good-sounding sales from small trade papers in a higher position on the list.

5. Information concerning the size and age of the estate

The older and the larger the estate, the better off you normally are. I like the estate sales that I attend to be at least forty years old, and preferably older, and I like to see it mentioned that the entire contents of the house will be sold, or that the house is packed, or that there is just too much merchandise to list. Ideally, I want to attend an estate sale where every item from that estate is going to be sold, not just selected or picked-over items. Some estates, such as farms, have been in the same family for many generations, and you can often find some very old and valuable items at these sales.

6. Is there a phone number listed?

It can be a very important factor if the ad for the estate sale includes a phone number. If the ad does include a phone number, then it's imperative that you call and get as much information as you can about the sale, and in particular what items they have for sale. Call regardless of what the ad states, even if the estate sale sounds poor, since you can never completely judge an estate sale strictly by what is written in the ad. When you contact the sellers, ask as many questions as you can, especially about specific items they might have for sale. Normally, you can get a good sense of the overall sale by finding out about a few of the items or classes of items they're selling. If they tell you they have magazines dated from the 1940s for sale, then it is likely that they will have other older items to sell. One of the most important questions you should ask the sellers is if they can make arrangements for you to come by the sale before the actual sale is scheduled to begin. Some sellers will flatly refuse your request, but frequently sellers will tell you that they don't mind; they just want to sell their possessions. You might also state that it is going to be difficult for you to get to the sale at the time it is being held. This may convince them to make arrangements for you to come early, fearing that they might lose out on a potential customer if they don't. You will be surprised how often this works, especially with a family-run estate sale. By attending the sale earlier, you have the distinct advantage of eliminating it completely from the list of sales that you are thinking about attending, along with the fact that you will have first choice of most of the items being sold. If they will not let you come early, then you should find out if they might be opening earlier than the time published in the ad on the day of the sale. If they say they might, or are not sure, then make sure that you arrive early to the sale. I have been to many sales that have opened earlier than the time published, and by arriving early, I have had my choice of the items being sold.

If there is no phone number listed, then you can at times find the phone number in a reverse directory, or if you know the name, find the number through directory assistance and attempt to contact them before the sale begins. The most important factor in calling the sellers is that you can determine the relative quality of the sale. If it sounds like it has little potential, then I eliminate it from my list. If it sounds like it might be a good sale, then I keep it on my list of estate sales that I might attend. I would like to reiterate how important it is to try to make arrangements to attend an estate sale before it actually starts. When you have your choice of any item that they have for sale, then your productivity and profits will go up exponentially. You can often make two to three times the amount of money by being the first or one of the first buyers at a sale.

7. Distance you have to travel to the estate sale

What is the distance to the sale? Make sure that estate sale doesn't involve a long drive. The distance is arbitrary, but I usually only attend estate sales that are less than a thirty-mile drive, unless of course the estate sale sounds exceptionally promising. It helps if you live near or in a larger city, as more estate sales will be available for you to choose from. Obviously, if the sale is too far away or will take me too long to get to, I usually eliminate it from my list.

8. What time and day of the week does the sale begin?

As alluded to earlier, the day and time of the sale can be very important. Often, you will find that there is only one sale starting on a particular day and time. When this is the case, the decision is made for you. When possible, I especially like to attend sales that begin on off-days and off-hours, and I have even gone as far as to change my schedule to attend them. There are normally fewer buyers to compete with, making the sale much more profitable.

Example

As I mentioned earlier, by using this list of items to evaluate all the estate-sale listings I have gathered, I am usually able to narrow my list of potentially good sales to about two or three.

An example of an estate-sale listing from a newspaper is given below. Usually the lists are much longer, and the demarcations not always so apparent. But you can usually get a pretty good idea which estate sales will likely be the most profitable, and you will be able to narrow the number of estate sales that you are interested in down to two or three sales. Of the following, which sale would you pick to attend?

> ESTATE SALE, BAKERSTOWN. Saturday, Dec. 3, 8 AM–4 PM, 2546 East Pike Street in Timberly Estates. 4-poster bed, loveseat, end tables, new refrigerator, TVs, VCR, collectibles, kitchen, dishes, printer, computer, bicycles, trunk, sweeper, women's clothing. Other good stuff. Silver Estate Sales, 411-999-5555.

> FANTASTIC ESTATE SALE. Sat. and Sun., Dec. 3 and 4, 7:30 AM– 3:30 PM, 3776 Shenago Street, New Brighton. Government forfeiture. Exquisite new living room, dining room, and two bedroom suites. Large screen TVs, Christmas items, 2002 Toyota Celica, tools, riding mower, tons unlisted. www.johnsestatesales.com.

> ESTATE SALE. Sat. and Sun., Dec. 3 and 4, 9:00 AM until? Much household, Little Tykes toys, new women's and men's clothing, refrigerator, stove, furniture, electric dryer and washer, games, much more. No early birds. Washington Crossing Townhouses, #4112.

> ESTATE SALE. Sat. and Sun., Dec. 3 and 4, 8 AM–4 PM, 173 Elm Street, Manchester section of the city. Complete contents of a large house, many antiques, books, 1930s GE radio, lot of old glassware and magazines, house to be torn down, nice large mantelpiece, too much to list. Third street past the Manchester Bridge. 305-555-1234.

> ESTATE SALE. Fri., Sat, Sun., Dec. 2–Dec. 4, 124 Carson Street. Contents of old bakery and house, closed in 1987, to settle family estate, tons of items, too much to list, a lot of antique furniture. Ovens, display cases. Some coins. 9 to 3. Bring pickup truck.

The first three ads can probably be eliminated from consideration because of the locations (one is a condominium, and the other two have newer-sounding addresses), and by the items they have listed. (Most of the items are newer items, and they have listed some items that have very little value at all, such as clothing.) You can also get an idea how good they might be, since professionals are running two of them. I would, however, call the first estate sale and look up the other sale on the Web site to be sure that I was not missing anything. The fourth and fifth ads both qualify as potentially profitable estate sales, and I would probably attend them both, since they open on different days. I would definitely arrive early to both of them. I would also call the fourth estate sale and find out more details, including whether they will open early. If they had both started on the same day, I would probably drive by the fourth estate sale to get a better idea of what kind of sale it might be. The number-one ad out of the five is the last ad. This is a sale that I would almost certainly attend. It has great potential. I would also drive by the sale, maybe more than once, and I would definitely arrive very early. Old businesses are always potentially good sales.

It is not always easy to identify which estate sale is likely to be the most profitable. It is usually easy to eliminate many of the estate sales from your list, but in my experience, there are always at least two or three that sound equally enticing. In this case, you have to either flip a coin or use your own intuition, or you can increase your odds by actually driving by the house where the estate sale is going to be held. This can be beneficial in a number of ways.

The drive-by

You have done your work and have picked out two or three estate sales that sound interesting, but you are unable to decide which one is the best. Instead of relying on chance, it may be a good idea to drive by the house before the sale. This can serve a number of purposes. If it's not that far away, I like to drive by the house in the afternoon or evening of the day before the sale. This is the most likely time that the sellers will be at the house preparing for the sale. Often there are sellers present at the house, and you can get the opportunity to look around at the items they might be selling. And if you're lucky and convincing enough, they may let you look through the house and purchase some of the items. Even if they won't, you can get a good idea of what items are for sale and where they might be located.

Most of the time, it is possible to get a good idea of how old the estate is just by looking at the house. Older estates tend to have older-appearing houses. This is not to say that the house itself is old, or that it's readily apparent by the style and construction of the house and by the neighborhood in which the house is located. As mentioned earlier, an old house does not necessarily mean that it's going to be an old estate, but often you can get some idea how old the estate might be by just looking at the house and its surroundings. If the curtains hanging in the windows look old, if the paint around the windows and eaves is well worn, if the fixtures (lawn ornaments, light fixtures, mailbox) all look old, then you may get the impression that the estate is old. When houses are sold, they are often remodeled, repaired, or updated. If it looks like it might need a lot of cosmetic repairs, then it might very well be an older estate. If it's possible, I normally walk around the house and attempt to get close enough to look through the windows. You can often see some of the items they are going to be selling. Children's items in the yard, such as a swing set or toys, almost always indicate that the estate is newer. If there are neighbors around, I try to get information from them about the estate and the upcoming sale. Many times they can give you the entire history of the house, who lived there and for how long, and even what items they may be selling. If you are not satisfied with what you have learned or seen, then you can eliminate the sale from your list and go to one of the other sales. I have recently been more inclined to drive by the house the day before the sale is to start. Recently, I have found that many listings have been overstated. It sounds like it will be an excellent sale, but when you arrive at the sale, you find that there is really nothing much of value, and that the ad was probably written in the hope of attracting more buyers. You don't want to miss a good sale simply because of the way the ad reads. This is also true with listings that say very little. If I am uncertain about an ad because of lack of information, but believe that it might hold potential, I will often attempt to drive by the house.

Alternate sites

Once you have determined which sale you are going to attend, the next step is to pick an alternate site, preferably near the first site. You can use this as a backup in case the first sale looks like it will not be profitable, or you can use it as a site to attend in the afternoon, when the prices on items will be reduced. Prices are typically cut in half in the afternoon. If you get there a little before noon, you can look around and begin to collect items at half-price. In the afternoon, I often negotiate more aggressively with sellers to get a price even lower than fifty percent. Toward the end of an estate sale, sellers can become desperate to sell their items, and you can often get some outstanding bargains if you negotiate, especially if you put together a collection of items to buy, sellers often do not want to lose a large sale, and they will cut their prices even more.

It can sometimes be of value to return to a sale where you have found that most of the items have initially been overpriced. Many times at these sales, a lot of valuable items go unsold and are still available at half the price in the afternoon.

What to buy

Once you have determined which estate sales you are going to attend, you can move on to the next phase of a productive sale. The next step is to ask yourself which items do you really want to buy. Which items at estate sales are likely to afford you the most profit? Although this is far from a black-and-white issue, in the following chapter I have outlined some general rules and guidelines and some broad classifications of items that should be looked for and purchased at estate sales. Although you can make money on almost any item you buy (if the price is right), I will attempt to define items that are likely to bring the highest profits. I believe that you should not buy an item unless you expect to make very close to a one-hundred percent profit, and preferably a lot more.

3

Knowing Which Items to Buy

Before you actually attend an estate sale, you should have a general idea of what items you actually want to buy. In this chapter, I will attempt to give a general overview of items that you are likely to encounter at estate sales and tell how to determine which items are likely to bring the most profit when resold. A specific list of items would be endless, but in most cases, it's easier to look at items in more general terms. Initially, I will list some very broad physical characteristics that should be taken into account when buying any items. After that, I will list certain broad classes of valuable items that are common finds at estate sales, and lastly I will list some specific areas of collecting that are important to keep in mind. The decision of which items to buy is not written in stone, and you can make a case for buying almost any item, especially if the price is right. I have, however, tried to focus my discussion on items that I believe are likely to produce a high profit margin and to eliminate those items that I feel are too difficult to sell or have little resale value.

One basic tenet I believe is important is that you should attempt to try to learn a little about a lot of different areas of valuables and collectibles, and try not to get bogged down with learning a lot about any one specific area of collecting. This is important for the obvious reason that you will be called on to identify the ballpark value of many different items at estate sales, not just one specific item. You should be prepared to judge the value of almost any item that you find at an estate sale. It is enough to know that Roseville pottery is valuable and very collectible; it is not necessary to know the actual rarity or value of the particular vase you have found. It would help, but it is impractical to attempt to learn everything about every item that you might encounter. By concentrating on one area of collecting, you are likely to overlook valuable items in other areas of collecting. Buyers do tend to gravitate to their areas of interest, and estate sales can be more exciting when you are looking for specific items, but I believe it is more valuable to have a working knowledge of a lot of different categories of antiques and collectibles. When it comes to estate sales, knowing a little about a lot is better than knowing a lot about a little.

The four basic physical aspects of an item that should be considered before you purchase an item are as follows:

1. The item should be old. "Old" is a relative term, but this generally means that the item should be at least forty years old, and preferably much older. Most items made before the mid-1960s were not produced in the quantities that they were after that period. Manufacture numbers started to go up exponentially after the sixties, making the items much more common and less valuable. Also, the number of collectors went up exponentially after the sixties, and many items were actually hoarded by collectors. A good example is baseball cards. Baseball cards dated before 1965 are generally a lot more valuable than those made at a later date. A box of Topps cards from 1960 would be worth thousands of dollars, but a box from the late seventies or early eighties is worth very little; as a matter of fact, they are often impossible to sell. In general, newer items are just too plentiful and have been collected too aggressively to attempt to make a profit on any of them. There are newer items that you can make money with, such as jewelry, but the price has to be right, and usually they are valuable not because of their age or rarity, but because of their intrinsic value.

Determining how the age of an item is not always simple. Many items have been reproduced and made to look old. To the naked eye, it is sometimes impossible to tell an authentic item from a recent reproduction. At the end of this chapter, I have listed some clues that will hopefully help you to determine the age of an object.

2. Most items should be smaller items. Normally this means nothing larger than a breadbox. There are many exceptions to the rule, but most of the time I try to adhere to this rule. The main reason is that larger items, although sometimes more valuable in offering a greater profit margin, frequently become a logistics nightmare. Trying to move, store, deliver, or mail a larger item sometimes can be too costly and time-consuming. How can you really manage something as large as an antique sideboard, regardless of its value, unless you are actually in the furniture business? I have passed on many valuable larger items at bargain prices just because they were too much of a management problem. Smaller items, on the other hand, are much easier to manage, and are much more attractive than larger items if you look at the ratio of profit to size. You can make $30 or more on something as small as a postage stamp. And although you can make $300 or more on a dresser, the time and effort involved can be very daunting. You also put more money at risk by buying a larger item. You will normally pay significantly more for larger items than you do for smaller items, and if you are unable to sell the item, you could lose your large investment.

3. Most items should be in good to excellent condition. The items don't need to be in mint condition, but they definitely should not have any major damage or easily noticeable flaws. I don't buy broken or cracked items, or any items that have parts missing, or incomplete sets of items. The value on most of these items is limited, and it's not worth taking the risk, and it can be costly to restore them to salable condition. In general, a buyer wants items that are in good, undamaged condition. If the damage is minor and the item displays well, then I will probably still consider buying it. You might also consider buying damaged items that are rare. The rarer the item, the more damage you can generally accept. Most items can be repaired to a condition of acceptability. Older items that still display well should probably be purchased if the price is right and the damage is minimal. The natural aging process *(e.g., the natural "foxing" or discoloration that occurs with older paper items)* should not really be considered damage, even though at times it may lower the value. I also don't normally buy repaired items, unless the repair is slight, or again if the item is rare. You should also be aware that if you don't inspect an item thoroughly, you might not realize that a part is completely missing. The item looks perfect, what's left of it; the problem is that it's not all there. I recently bought an item that looked complete but actually had a piece missing, but I didn't notice it because the missing piece was not obvious. It turned a $50 item into an item not worth more than $5. If I had looked more closely, I would have realized that the item was not complete.

4. A fourth consideration that is important (but somewhat subjective) is the displayability of an item. An item can meet the first three conditions, but if the item is not displayable or collectible, then it might not be worth much. An old doorknob in perfect condition has little value if it does not have some collectibility or displayability. Would the item look nice sitting on a shelf? Glass and pottery items, in particular, often fall into this category. Would it fit in with a collection of items? People collect all sorts of topical items: birds, lighthouses, dogs, etc. Actually, there are few displayable items that aren't collected; barbed wire even has collectors. Is it an item that would display well by itself, such as an unusual ashtray or wall hanging? Unusual items should always be considered as a potential buy. They tend to be conversation pieces, and often are relatively rare.

Any items that meet these four conditions of being older, smaller, in good condition, and displayable should be considered for purchase.

Classes of items

The following are classes of items that you should search for and consider buying at an estate sale. These are items that you normally encounter at most estate sales. As I mentioned earlier, there are many exceptions, and there is some overlap of categories, but in general, over ninety percent of the items that should be considered for purchase will fall into one of the following categories.

1. Ephemera: paper items, advertising items, magazines, etc. The definition of ephemera is any item with a short life or duration. This includes almost all paper items, advertising items, calendars, etc. It also includes any items that people tended to throw away or probably should have thrown away when they were finished with them—items that were intended for a definite time period. For example, political buttons generally are designed to be used for about three or four months prior to an election, and then discarded. Old boxes, matchbooks, and gum and candy wrappers can all be valuable items, because they were items that normally were discarded. This category also includes old cans and bottles. Some of these items can be extremely valuable and are often overlooked at estate sales. This is one of the reasons it is important to check shelves and cupboards, especially in the basement, where older cans and bottles are often stored. If you find an item that you feel should have been thrown away a long time ago, then you should consider buying that item.

2. Small collectibles: jewelry, toys, stamps, political items, coins, memorabilia, etc. This category includes any items that are heavily collected, such as gold and silver items, and any other small metal items: tokens, watches, pens, etc. Look for jewelry that is ten-carat, sixteen-carat, or twenty-four-carat gold, or sterling silver. I generally consider buying marked gold and silver jewelry, because this usually means that the item is a quality item, and if it contains any type of setting, then it is likely to be a stone or gem of higher quality. Avoid items marked "nickel silver," or "gold and silver plated," or "gold filled." All toys should be considered for purchase if they are at least forty years old. Most of these toys will be metal, but there are some older rubber and plastic toys that are valuable. I also consider newer toys that are still in their original packaging. Strongly consider buying any older US or foreign coins if the price is reasonable, and also any older uncanceled stamps. Canceled stamps, for the most part, are not valuable.

3. Photographs, prints, paintings, posters, maps, etc. Always look at what's hanging on the walls. You will often find interesting prints and paintings. Some prints are worth thousands of dollars, and prints are very commonly found at estate sales. On any older prints, check for copyright dates, the printer's name, and any signatures. Paintings should be judged by the quality of the painting; most of the time this simply means that the painting looks like the subjects or objects portrayed in the painting; *i.e.,* the people in the painting should look like real people, not stick figures. A good-quality oil painting, whether signed or unsigned, should be considered as a possible item to purchase. Paintings can be very valuable, and most paintings at estate sales are unidentified.

4. Ceramic, pottery, and glass items, especially items that are marked. Items that are marked are typically more valuable than unmarked items. If you can identify the maker, the items are usually more valuable and more collectible, and thus much easier to resell. Be aware, however, that forged maker's marks can be added to an item, and this seems to be especially true with popular collectible items. With ceramic, glass, and pottery items, it is always very important to check for chips and cracks. Chips can most reliably be detected by running your hand across the surface of the item. Cracks and repaired areas normally fluoresce under black light.

5. Fixtures. If the house is to be remodeled or demolished, you can frequently find valuable fixtures at estate sales. Many times the seller is unaware they are even there. This category includes switch plates, doorknobs, light fixtures, etc. Look at the walls, ceilings, and floors at all estate sales. I know of one person who found thousands of dollars' worth of Van Briggle tiles surrounding an old fireplace.

A basic principle to remember when attending estate sales—one that is not frequently appreciated—is that you are likely to only find items from a definite period of time. This means that most items you will find at an estate sale will be the age of that estate. If it is a seventy-year-old estate, then most of the items will be seventy years old or newer. There may be some older items that were bought or had been in the family for a longer time, but in general, items will be no older than the age of the estate. Most estate sales involve estates that are no older than about seventy or eighty years.

What does this mean? It means that most items you find will be within that time period, and it is unlikely that you will find many items older than seventy years. Toys are a good example. Cast-iron toys were very popular around the turn of the century, but you very seldom find any original cast-iron toys at estate sales today. They have all been put into collections or bought long ago by antique dealers. There are plenty of reproductions (almost all the ones you find), but very few authentic cast-iron toys. This is important to remember, and it cuts across all fields of collecting. If you find an item that falls out of this age range, you have to seriously question its authenticity. Some examples of items that are not found much anymore are oil lamps, butter molds, and hatpins. You may find them, but they are becoming more rare. This principle is important in that it's not really all that productive or necessary to concentrate on learning about items that are much older than seventy years, since you are so unlikely to find them at many estate sales.

I should also point out that age does not always determine value. There is a certain window when certain items become very popular and collectible and thus very valuable, but when this window closes, the value of the items tends to fall. This is called the "thirty-year rule"; loosely stated, items become collectible and valuable about thirty years after they were originally popular. This is because the children from that time are now adults wanting to buy the items they had as children. Once this time period ends, however, the demand also wanes. A good example of this is character dolls. Shirley Temple and Charlie McCarthy, famous characters from the thirties, were at one time very valuable, but since about the seventies, their value has continued to fall. Now, more valuable items are likely to be Roy Rogers and Superman items from the sixties and seventies. Even these items have begun to fall in value. Items from earlier generations become less valuable because there are fewer collectors searching for those items. This rule is important to know, but it is not important enough to make you ignore an older item because you believe it is no longer as valuable or as collectible as it once was. Regardless of the age of an item, there are still some collectors out there willing to buy these items. It's also a reason for buying mint-condition toys in their original packaging from the seventies, eighties, or nineties. Most of these toys will become more valuable in the coming years. Some are already very valuable; Strawberry Shortcake has become the Barbie of the 2000s.

The following is a list of more specific items that you will frequently encounter at estate sales. Again, most of the items should be at least thirty or forty years old and in good condition before you consider buying them. I have found that it is very helpful to purchase a reference book that lists the most popular areas of collecting. I look through this book frequently to become familiar with all the different types of collectibles, and I always keep it handy so I can look up items I might need to identify.

1. Advertising items (anything even remotely related to advertising)

2. Architectural items

3. Automobile-related items (license plates, maps, etc.)

4. Baseball (cards, gloves, bats, etc.)

5. Beatles (anything vintage Beatle, character collectibles)

6. Bottles (soda, beer, perfume, figural, label under glass, etc.)

7. Books (first edition with good dust covers, or illustrated children's books with nice covers)

8. Buttons (unusual, figural buttons, political, advertising, military, etc.)

9. Christmas (ornaments, displays, bulbs, etc.)

10. Cigarettes (packs, cards, lighters, ashtrays, etc.)

11. Circus (posters, buttons, toys, programs, etc.)

12. Coins (foreign, commemorative, or any coins)

13. Coca-Cola items (if they're older than 1970 and not reproductions)

14. Comic books (10¢, 12¢, 15¢, or 25¢, with good covers)

15. Cut glass (sharp-feeling glass that rings when you tap it due to its high lead content)

16. Disney (figures, plates, jewelry, etc.)

17. Dolls (especially character dolls in their original boxes)

18. Electrical (radios, portable televisions, clocks, etc.)

19. Ephemera (any paper items older than 1970, calendars, posters, postcards, empty candy boxes, even gum wrappers; if it should have been thrown away and wasn't, it's probably rare and worth money)

20. Fire department collectibles (extinguishers, helmets, etc.)

21. Fishing/hunting (poles, lures, decoys, etc.)

22. Games (TV-related; standard games like Clue, Monopoly, and Password are not usually that valuable, but all other games are valuable)

23. Gas station (giveaways, oilcans, etc.)

24. Glass (thick that glows under black light, or cut or marked; there are over 5,000 patterns of glass and counting)

25. Gold (anything marked 10–24K gold; nothing gold plated or gold filled)

26. Halloween (costumes, decorations, etc.)

27. Japan, Occupied Japan (anything marked as such)

28. Jewelry (quality jewelry, marked gold or silver; it helps if it has a maker's mark)

29. Kitchenware (unusual items, pie birds, string holders, cookie cutters, etc.)

30. Laundry (old soap boxes, pin holders, shaker bottles, irons, etc.)

31. Magazines (old with notable artwork covers; *i.e.,* Norman Rockwell, famous people, icons on cover, Marilyn Monroe, Mickey Mantle, etc.)

32. Medical (books, instruments, etc.)

33. Military (firearms, bayonets, scrip, medals, etc.)

34. Movies (anything movie-related: cards, posters, giveaways, etc.)

35. Music (sheet music with nice covers, instruments, etc.)

36. Paintings, lithographs, prints, etc.

37. Photography (old photos, tintypes, cameras, etc.)

38. Political (anything political: pins, posters, etc.)

39. Posters (most posters are of some value, regardless of their purpose)

40. Radio (radios; clock radios are usually less valuable)

41. Railroad (lanterns, schedules, etc.)

42. Records (good covers, sleeves, rare labels, etc.)

43. Sewing (button cards, needle cards, buttons, etc.)

44. Silver (anything marked "sterling silver," not silver plated or nickel silver)

45. Sports (cards, old equipment, etc.)

46. Stamps (older US and foreign stamps; uncanceled or unhinged are better)

47. Store-related (displays, advertising, giveaways, etc.)

48. Telephone-related (old phones, directories, etc.)

49. Tools—primitive, marked, wooden construction, i.e. Stanley planes, etc.

50. Toys (any toys, newer toys in original boxes)

51. Trains (any Lionel or American Flyer trains and accessories)

52. Watches (pocket watches; early and even newer well-constructed, non-battery watches; newer designer watches by Swatch, Fossil, etc.)

Items that are unusual and display well should be considered, as should any hot items, and all items in their original packaging. Items in multiple quantities, like postcards, offer the ability to multiply your profits; you can purchase the entire lot and then resell them individually.

You should always attempt to identify reproduction or fantasy items. This task, however, is not always easy to accomplish. Today, many items are made from original molds with original markings and artificially aged. I recently went into a toy store and found a new robot for sale that was identical to an older model that is worth thousands of dollars. Even the box had scuff marks applied to make it look authentic. Even under black light it looked good, until I found a corner of the box where the underlying paper was exposed. This area of the box lit up very brightly. I have found that many of the most highly reproduced items are those items of popular brands that are highly collectible, such as Coca-Cola and Marx. If, as the maxim states, you find an item that looks too good to be true, then it probably isn't. If you have any doubts about an item, you should always check it under a black light. I might have seriously considered buying this item if I had found it at an estate sale instead of at a toy store.

The following are groups of items that you will find at almost every estate sale. I tend to avoid these items initially, until I have inspected most of the other items in the house. I do, however, examine these items thoroughly on a later trip through the house. These are items that I don't frequently buy, but as always, there are many exceptions.

1. Books and magazines. I tend to stay away from books. Most of the time, there are many books at estate sales, and to inspect them all can be very time-consuming. But more importantly, most books have very little resale value unless they are rare first editions with good dust covers, or are very old books. Most books are not rare. You can, however, look for books that have dust covers. A dust cover is the original paper cover that was placed around the book to protect the binding, but many have been lost or destroyed over the years. Dust covers are easy to pick out on a shelf containing many books. I look at the books with dust covers to see if they are first editions, avoiding the very common book-club editions. If it is a first edition with a dust cover, then I consider buying the book. Even most of these books will not be of great value. I will also occasionally buy older books with colorful, expressive graphics on their dust jackets, especially children's books. If nothing else, they display well.

Magazines, especially the newer ones, are not usually that valuable. Ninety percent of the value of a magazine is in the cover. If you don't recognize the person on the cover, then it's probably not worth much. If it has Marilyn Monroe, Mickey Mantle, or Elvis, or it has a Norman Rockwell cover, then I might consider buying the magazine if it is in good condition. You should always consider buying any older or unusual magazines from before 1950. These magazines are often referred to as pulp magazines. You can also identify the age of most magazines by the price printed on the cover. Ten-cent comic books and magazines priced at 25¢ or less should be considered for purchase.

2. Clothes and accessories. I don't normally buy clothes; most aren't old enough, and there are not a whole lot of collectors. Vintage clothes can be valuable, but they are also inherently prone to major condition problems, which are often difficult to rectify (moth holes, stains, dry rot, etc.). It is also difficult to determine a valuable designer item (such as Gucci) from a cheap reproduction. My wife collects Vera scarves, which are frequent finds at estate sales. There are some rare designer clothes that are valuable, like Lucille Ball dresses, but they are so rare as to not be much of a consideration. I occasionally look at the tags on the clothes, if time permits. You can sometimes find an unusual label. You can, however, often find some great bargains on leather or Lucite purses, belts, fur coats, or other accessories. My wife frequently finds excellent buys in this area, and she recently purchasing a $500 fur coat for $25. As I mentioned earlier, clothes and accessories are items that I inspect later in the sale.

3. Records and albums. It seems as though no one ever threw away their albums, and so there are not many that are truly rare, and the rare albums or records are, as expected, very seldom found. Thus the value of most records and albums is marginal. Most collectors already possess the common albums, which makes it difficult to sell most of the albums or records that you buy. You will find records and albums at almost all estate sales; it is the one item that you're almost always guaranteed to find. I normally only buy records that have interesting picture sleeves and are in good condition. On the other hand, I very rarely buy any albums, regardless of the cover. Even most albums by famous musicians, such as Elvis Presley, have little resale value.

4. Kitchen-related items. I tend to stay away from kitchen items unless they are unusual. There's usually a ton of kitchen utensils and other kitchen items (pots, pans, etc.) at estate sales, but very few are valuable. Occasionally you might find an unusual timer, or a pie bird, or a string holder, but unless you head to the kitchen at the start of the sale, you are unlikely to find anything of real value by the time you get around to searching the kitchen. Many of the more valuable kitchen items are located in the dining room anyway.

5. Tools and garage items. I usually don't buy tools, unless they are unusual or older tools. If you can't readily identify a tool's function, it is an unusual tool, and older tools can usually be identified by how they were constructed. Good-quality tools or tools that contain wooden parts are usually older. Tools that have a manufacturer's mark also tend to be more valuable. Stanley planes can be very valuable, but unless you are very knowledgeable in this area, it is often somewhat difficult to determine which ones are truly valuable. Most tools hold little value. Tools are another class of item that I only consider buying after I have made at least one trip through the house.

6. Collectible items. I normally don't buy items that were specifically made for the collector's market, such as collector plates, figurines, cookie jars, or the countless other collectible items marketed through magazines and television ads. These items, for the most part, go down in value over time. The buyers are made to believe that the items are great investments that will, in time, go up in value, when in reality, the opposite is usually the case. I also do not usually buy newer sports collectibles, such as cards, bats, plaques, glasses, or autographed sports items. For the most part, these items are just too plentiful. I recently attended an estate sale where one whole room was filled with collectible plates; hundreds of plates that had initially sold for between $25 to $50 (and some higher) were now priced at $3 each. I did not see one plate being sold while I was at the sale. Collectible items generally do not hold their value well, regardless of what the manufacturers claim, and most of them are difficult to resell.

7. Furniture. Most furniture is too large to deal with, unless you have the ways and means to transport and store the items. You can frequently find smaller pieces of furniture that are worth buying and will not be a management problem. You should, however, have some idea how to judge the quality and determine the age of any furniture you are contemplating buying.

Determining age

The following are some things you should look for when trying to determine the age of an object. It can be normally assumed that most items at an estate sale are older or are period items, but you should still be on the alert for any items that may be newer reproductions. When attempting to determine the age of an item, the most important thing is to inspect the item very closely, think about what you have observed, and then inspect it again.

1. Look for any markings on the item. At times, this is the most important part of determining the age of an object. This includes any marks, regardless of what they are. Mold numbers, maker's marks, addresses, phone numbers, country of origin, and patent numbers are just some of the various markings that you should look for to help you determine the age of an item.

a) Patent numbers. The patent number can tell you the age of an item, or at least when it was patented. The first seven-digit patent number was issued around 1910, so almost all six-digit numbers indicate that the item was made in the 1800s. With objects that have a seven-digit patent number, you can determine the approximate year the item was patented by taking the first two numbers in the patent number and doubling them. For example, if the number begins with 20, then the item was patented around 1940. If the first two numbers are 32, then the object has an approximate patent year of 1964. This is, however, only a very loose approximation of the patent year. Remember that patent dates do not always indicate when the item was made, only when it was patented.

Most new items are not marked with a patent number. There are exceptions, though; Pez dispensers almost always contain a patent number, for example.

b) Phone numbers. Items with low phone numbers are usually older. Items containing two-digit phone numbers usually were made around the 1920s, three-digit numbers indicate the 1930s, four-digit numbers indicate the 1940s, and so on. This is only a loose approximation of age. A phone number that includes letters to indicate the exchange is also usually older; *e.g.,* BR-7-1234. These numbers were issued in the fifties and sixties. Obviously, numbers with area codes or 800 numbers are newer items.

c) Country of origin. Some items will be marked with older or former names of countries, or countries that no longer exist. "Nippon" is how most Japanese items were marked before the 1920s. Yugoslavia and Siam are countries that no longer exist, and an item marked as such may be an older item.

d) Addresses. Look for unusual state abbreviations, like O. for Ohio or Penna. for Pennsylvania. These were used prior to the mid-1960s.

e) Zones, Zip codes, and bar codes. Zones were used between 1944 and 1964 (Pittsburgh 4, Chicago 18, etc.). They were replaced with five-digit Zip codes in 1964, and the nine-digit Zip code debuted in the 1990s. Bar code first appeared in 1974, and Web addresses became popular in the late 1990s. Being familiar with these mile markers can help you identify the age of an object.

f) Maker's marks. These are painted-on marks, impressions, stickers, etc. Remember, however, that stickers and marks can be added. I always gently attempt to lift a sticker, just enough to determine if there is a color change beneath. Normally the area beneath any sticker that has been in place for a number of years is lighter, unoxidized. An item's age can often be determined by identifying the maker's mark.

g) Marks I avoid. I don't buy items with bar codes or Web addresses. I don't know how many times I have picked up an item that looks old, only to find that it has a bar code pasted to the bottom. I also don't buy items that I believe to be reproductions. These are typically items with popular brand names or makers that have no other evidence of age. (I will come back to this area later in the book.) I also tend not to buy items that are unmarked. I generally do not buy items marked Hong Kong, China, or Taiwan; most of these items were made after 1975. I only buy items made after 1970 if they are quality or highly collectible items, such as toys in their original packaging. I recently bought a Hot Wheels set from the early seventies in the original box for $5 that sold for over $1,000.

h) Price tags. Many items still retain their original price tags. Items with prices of 10¢ and 29¢ are usually older. Items that are worth a lot more than their price tags state are obviously older.

2. Examine the item for its materials and the process that was used to manufacture it. Items made of unusual materials such as Bakelite, celluloid, or Lucite are usually old. Conversely, if an item is made of plastic and not metal, then you can assume that it's likely a newer item. There are older plastic items, but plastic became much more popular as a material in the sixties. You should also check to see if the item was constructed using an older manufacturing process. Many older toys, for example, were put together using metal flaps to hold the parts in place. Today, most items are put together using welds or small rivets. This can easily be determined just by examining the item. Older metal items were also decorated using a process called tin lithography, in which the paint is added directly to the tin surface. Today, decorations are applied as decals. Friction toys and wind-up toys were common in the thirties and forties, but were not common after the sixties. Older glass was often hand-cut. All of these factors should be considered when attempting to determine the age of an item. Age is often difficult to determine when you first begin buying items at estate sales, but it becomes rather easy as you become more experienced. I should state, however, that many newer items have been manufactured to look old; wear and the discoloration and other effects of aging can be added to objects, and you can find wind-up toys and friction toys at most toy stores today. This practice just makes determining the age of an object that much more difficult.

3. Look for evidence of wear on the item. The wear on an item is particularly important in determining its age. Older items should possess normal wear patterns; *i.e.,* objects should show a loss of surface glaze or smoothness on all surfaces that come in contact with other objects, such as the base of a teapot that frequently rubs across the surface of a table. There should be noticeable wear on the bases of any older objects. If there is no wear, then you can assume it is probably a newer item. Surface wear is usually indicated by a wearing off of the glaze or surface covering, giving the area a different color or texture. The texture is usually rough to the touch, the appearance usually dull.

4. Look for signs of oxidation on the surface of the item. This is the natural aging process caused by the object's exposure to oxygen. Oxidation normally causes the item to lose its natural shine or luster, making it appear much duller than a newer item. If the item looks like it just came off a store shelf, then it should be considered a newer item until proven otherwise.

5. Look for signs of the natural aging of the object. Oxidation is part of the natural aging process, but you should also look for "crazing" in ceramic items and "foxing" in paper items.

If you still have any doubts about the age of an object, then it is best to examine the item under a black light. As I mentioned earlier, older glass items give off a greenish glow under black light, and newer paper (after the 1950s) fluoresces brightly under black light, as do repairs made to ceramic items.

The list of items that are worth buying is endless, but with time you can develop a good sense of which items hold the greatest value. Theoretically, you can make a profit on just about any item you buy, if the price is right. I should also emphasize that no item should ever be overlooked. Even an item that you initially feel has no value should be looked at carefully to make sure that you are not passing up something valuable. Some beat-up items such as books and sports items can actually be quite valuable. Some years ago, I bought a beat-up old baseball glove for $2 that sold for $150. You should also buy items that you like. If you like it, there's a good chance others will like it too.

You can theoretically determine the rough value of almost any item by two simple factors: the number of collectors versus the number of that particular item that exist. The more collectors and the rarer the item, the more valuable the item will be. Take, for instance, a 1908 Honus Wagner baseball card. It is a million-dollar card because there are fewer than ten original cards available to millions of collectors. Conversely, fewer collectors of a very common item make these items less valuable.

Now that you have determined which estate sale you are going to attend and have a general idea of the items that you will be looking for when you arrive at the sale, you can move on to the next step of a successful estate sale: preparing for and going to the sale.

Remember, estate sales are treasure hunts. You are searching for diamonds in the rough, and you will be surprised how often you will find a diamond.

4

The Day of the Estate Sale

Know where you're going

You have chosen the estate sale that you will be attending, and you have a general idea of the items you want to buy. The next important step is to make sure you have accurate directions to estate sale. Don't get lost; it could ruin all your plans. Even arriving late to a sale could be disastrous, because the most important time of any estate sale is the first hour. So the first step is to make sure that you have clear directions to the sale. I normally obtain directions online through one of the online mapping services, such as Mapquest. Online directions are generally very detailed and they offer the option to view any sections of the route that may be unfamiliar to you or difficult to follow from just the written directions. These maps are normally very accurate and easy to follow. The mapping services also give you the distance and the approximate drive time to your destination, which can be very helpful in planning when to start your journey. I always make a printed copy of the directions. The night before the sale, I normally go over the map to make certain that it is the right address and that I have a general idea where I'm going and what time I will need to leave.

I also occasionally use a detailed city street atlas to give me a better idea where the sale is with regard to other areas of the city. It often makes the directions much easier to follow if you know the general location of the sale.

It is important to know exactly where you are headed and about how long it might take to get there, since it's imperative that you arrive at the sale on time. As I already mentioned, arriving late to an estate sale can be a fatal mistake, ruining your chances of being one of the first to search the house for valuable items. I make sure that I have a copy of the driving directions with me before I leave for the estate sale.

What to bring

It's important to bring some containers you can use to carry all your items. I normally use a medium-sized cardboard box and a few shopping bags, which I put in the box. Even though there are usually cardboard boxes available at the sale, I bring my own, just in case there aren't any. The container should be large enough to hold a moderate number of small to medium-sized items, but not so large as to hinder you movement through the house and around other buyers. I also like the container to be small enough so that I can hold it under my arm, in case I need both hands to inspect an item. I also like to bring a couple of shopping bags, or a bag that I can carry over my shoulder. At most sales, one box is not enough, and I usually end up filling at least one box and two or three shopping bags. It can become very burdensome, but you need to make sure that you keep all your items with you until you pay for them and have them safely locked in you car. This may seem excessive, but it is too easy for items left behind to be watched by someone else (usually the sellers) to end up missing from your container. Many times, people will go through your items, thinking that they are still for sale, especially if the sellers get busy doing something else, which they commonly do.

Bring a flashlight and a magnifying glass small enough to carry in your pocket The light comes in handy in old, poorly lit houses, especially when you have to look into dark spaces or in attics and basements. The magnifying glass comes in handy when reading small print on the items you might want to buy. You should also bring a cell phone to use, in case you get lost on your way to the sale—or, more importantly, so that you can call someone to check on the value or authenticity of an item you have found at the sale. You don't want to pay a lot for an item, only to find out later that it is a cheap reproduction.

You should also bring a few "sold" tags to put on larger items that you might want to buy, but are too large to carry with you through the house. I normally put my name and phone number on the backs of the tags. If you put a "sold" tag on an item, make sure that you take the price tag off the item and keep it as proof that you're the person who actually placed the "sold" tag on the item. It also makes it more difficult for someone else to buy the item, because they won't know the item's actual price.

You should also dress appropriately, especially in the winter, for the long waits outside, but also in the summer, when the temperature inside an old house can be very hot and uncomfortable. Bring a cheap umbrella when it looks like it might rain. I keep one in the car all the time. That way, you can keep your place in line when it's raining. A word about the weather: Bad weather can make for good estate sales, especially during the winter, when there has been a recent snowstorm or when the temperature is uncomfortably cold, since many buyers will be unable or unwilling to fight the weather to attend the sale. If possible (and when safe), you should attempt to attend these estate sales. When the crowds are small, there's less competition, and you can often have your pick of the items at the sale. Some of my best sale experiences have occurred during bad weather conditions.

It also helps if you bring something to read while you're waiting. It makes the time go by a little faster. I normally take a newspaper to read while standing in line. The newspaper can also come in handy as packing material for any glass items you might buy. Instead of throwing the paper away when I've finished reading it, I just put it in the bottom of my container.

You should also make sure to bring enough cash with you to the sale. You never know exactly how much you might need. I usually make sure that I have about three hundred dollars. This is usually more than enough, but there have been occasions when I've run out of money and had to either find an ATM or write a check. Most sellers won't take a check, but most sellers will also hold items until you get back from the ATM. I take a personal check or two anyway, just in case they will accept a check.

It may seem mundane, but it is important to park legally when you arrive at the sale. Most estate sales are in residential areas, where the streets are narrow and on-street parking is frequently restricted. This normally might not be a problem, but with the unusually heavy traffic generated by a sale, it is not uncommon for the police to arrive at some point during the sale for traffic control. Park as close as possible to the sale, but park legally. Many times I have seen people lose their places in line before a sale starts or have to move their cars during the sale. I have also seen a whole street full of cars with parking tickets under their windshield wipers, and once I witnessed a car being towed off down the street.

Work in pairs

Two people can cover a house a lot more efficiently than one person, and I have found that I have been much more productive at estate sales when my wife has attended the sale with me. Since most valuable items are bought early in the sale, it make sense that two people going through the house in different directions will almost certainly find more valuable items. Two people also naturally have a broader knowledge of items that have value. It is also nice to have company at the sale, and to find items that you know the other person might be interested in buying.

Get to the sale early

The next important aspect of the estate sale is to always arrive early. I cannot emphasize this enough! If I had one piece of advice to give anyone about estate sales, it would be to arrive early. I like to arrive anywhere from thirty minutes to an hour before the sale is scheduled to start—no later than that, and earlier when possible. It may seem like a waste of time to arrive early to a sale to just stand there and wait in front of the house, but it can pay off in the long run, and seasoned buyers have learned the importance of arriving early. For starters, there will occasionally be valuable estate items for sale that are located on the porch. By arriving early, you can be one of the first people to search these items. At a recent estate sale, I found over $300 worth of old board games, glassware, and toys just sitting out on the front porch of the house. If I hadn't arrived early, I'm sure that the items would have been taken. If I find anything I want to buy on the porch or around the house at any estate sale, even before the sale starts, I pick it up and put it in my container. If you don't, someone else will.

By arriving early, you may also decide that the estate sale has so little potential that you still have enough time to get to your alternate choice of estate sales. This can be risky, though, since it actually may be worse than your first choice and you will likely not be one of the first buyers when you arrive at the second estate sale.

By far the most important reason for arriving early at an estate sale is that often, family (and even some professionals) will open the estate sale early. Families running estate sales will frequently open up when they feel they're done preparing for the sale, and even sometimes before they are through setting up, and families are almost always at the house early on the day of the sale to set up. If I'm one of the first people at an estate sale and I know they are inside setting up, I will knock on the door to let them know that I have arrived. Often they will open the door and let me in. If they do decide to open early, I want to make sure that I am there and don't miss this golden opportunity. I frequently get to roam around a house by myself for twenty to thirty minutes before anyone else arrives. By the time a crowd arrives, I'm already leaving with most of the valuable items.

Even if they do not open the estate sale early, you will at least be one of the first people in line. Being first in line, or at least one of the first people in line, is important for two reasons. First, you will have first shot at many more items than buyers farther back in line will have, and by being close to the door, you can often get the opportunity to question the sellers as they're preparing for the sale, asking them what items they have for sale or where certain items might be located. With the information you obtain, you can often go directly to the items you know are valuable. The second advantage of arriving early and being first in line is that occasionally the people running the estate sale (particularly professionals) will give out numbers or have a sign-in sheet in order to let only so many buyers into the house at one time. By arriving early, you are able to establish your position in line and assure that you will be one of the first buyers inside the house. I'm always a little nervous if I'm any farther back than the fifteenth person in line; fifteen seems to be the lowest number of people that sellers will let in the house at any one time. Sometimes they will let in more, but you can never be certain. I have, in the past, had to wait until others have gone through the house, because my number in line was greater than the number of people they were letting in. This is a distinct advantage if you're in the first group of people let into the house, and a distinct disadvantage if you're not. To have the privilege of roaming around the house leisurely, looking for valuable items with just fourteen other people for as long as you want, gives you the opportunity to find, most of the time, a majority of the valuable items available.

Arriving early also gives you a cushion of time, in case you get lost. I have occasionally had a difficult time finding a sale, even when I had detailed and explicit directions. By leaving early, I have a cushion of time to fall back on if I get lost. If you remember one important thing about any estate sale, it is to arrive early!

I would also pretty much ignore the statement *No Early Birds* when it appears in an ad for an estate sale. It is an unreliable statement. I have seen many sales where "early birds" were in fact let into the house long before the sale was scheduled to begin. So arrive early, regardless of what the ad states.

Know which door you're going to enter

You should know which door the sellers are going to open to let the buyers in when the sale starts. This might seem mundane, but waiting in a line for an hour at the wrong door can be very disheartening, especially when you realize that a whole line of people has already started streaming through another door at the back of the house.

When you arrive

Once you have arrived at the sale and established your position in line, you should attempt to make a quick trip around the house, to look through any accessible windows and to locate any outbuildings that might contain estate-sale items; garages and storage sheds often contain valuable items. Make sure you ask if they contain any estate items when the estate sale opens. It's important to find out early in the sale if there are items for sale in these buildings; if possible, get a general description of what these items are. If there are potentially valuable items in other buildings, I will search them as soon as I make my first trip through the main house.

You should also look for any other items that might be valuable around the house and on the porches: old thermometers, milk boxes, mailboxes, lawn ornaments, etc. If you can see through any windows, try to locate any valuable items. Often you can look through a window and see the entire contents of a room. If you find a room that contains many valuable items, then you can head directly to the room when the sale starts.

You can also check the ad to determine where it might be best to start your search. If the ad states that the sale contains a lot of collectible glass, then you might want to start your search in a room where most collectible glass is found, like the dining room. If the ad says there are a lot of old Christmas or holiday decorations, then you might want to start your search in the basement. If they list a specific item that you are particularly interested in, then ask one of the sellers where the item is located when you enter the house. As I mentioned before, it can be very helpful to talk to any sellers who might be around before the sale starts, and ask them about the location of any of the items that were mentioned in the ad, or any items you are interested in buying.

If you can't determine where any of the items that you might be interested in are, and the sweep around the house has not helped you decide which rooms you are going to go to first, then it is up to you where to start your search. There is no hard and fast rule to follow about where the most valuable items are most likely to be located; I've gone straight to them, and I have missed them completely. There is no way to determine, with any degree of certainty, which rooms hold all the treasures. In my experience, the living room is high on the list, but unfortunately this room seems to be the most crowded early in the sale. There is a loose order of rooms that I tend to follow in searching through the house. I initially start with the living room and dining room, and any other downstairs rooms other than the kitchen and bathroom, and then I search the bedrooms and other upstairs rooms. When I am done going through those rooms, I search the basement and garage. If there are any other buildings with estate items, I search them next. Kitchens and bathrooms normally hold very few valuable items, so I tend to search them later; however, I have found very valuable items in every room, including bathrooms. If there is an accessible attic, which is not all that uncommon in older houses, I frequently search this room first, since many older items are often stored there.

If you are knowledgeable about glass, then it might make sense to start in the dining room, where most of the glass is usually located. If you specialize in tools, then you will obviously want to start your search in the garage or basement. This decision ultimately becomes one of personal preference, and it depends a lot on the expertise of the buyer. Whatever the order you use, it is more important that you thoroughly search every room in the house for valuable items.

The three-pass system

Over the years, I have developed a routine of going through houses at estate sales. I call it the "three-pass system," since I essentially make three separate passes through the house, and many times, a fourth. I believe that in principle it works well and is better than other systems. This routine will maximizes your ability to find and buy as many valuable antiques and collectibles as possible.

The first pass: smash and grab

The most important time of an estate sale is the first thirty minutes! Most valuable items at an estate sale are bought within the first thirty minutes. This is the time when you have to aggressively seek out the items that you believe are valuable. Run, pass up slow-moving people, force yourself into an area, maneuver between people—whatever it takes to get to the items that you want to look at or buy. Short of knocking someone over, you should try to make your way though the house as quickly as possible. The basic principle of the first trip though the house is to move as quickly as possible through the house, attempting to locate and take with you as many valuable items that you can find.

I don't spend any time inspecting, analyzing, or thinking about the actual worth of any specific item. If it's valuable or looks valuable, or I think that it may be valuable, I take the item and place it in my container and move on to the next item, knowing that later I will make my final decision about whether I actually want to buy the item. I definitely do not spend any time making a decision about any item during my first pass through the house, and I don't leave any items behind, thinking that I will return later to make my decision. The item just gets put into my container. And there is no rule that says that you can't pick up an item and take it with you, even if you are not certain you want to buy it. I have often looked like a pack mule, carrying items through the house before making my final decision about buying the items. For example, if I find a stack of postcards that are individually priced, I don't stop and look through them one at a time to choose the ones I want; instead, I take the whole stack, put it in my box, and look through them later when I have more time. If I stopped to look at which cards I actually wanted, I would be wasting valuable time, and most likely squandering the opportunity to find other valuable items in another part of the house. I will look much closer at these items later, when I have more time and when I'm sure that I've made it through the house and have gathered up all the items that might be worth buying.

There is also something to be said for not making quick decisions, since you are unlikely to notice small flaws, damaged items, or other problems with an item when you make a hasty decision. If I come to a larger item that I'm interested in buying, I pull off the price tag and put a "sold" tag on it. I can always change my mind and put the price tag back on the item later. I don't use the "sold" tags excessively, but if an item is just too large for me to carry around the house or will get in my way, then I put a "sold" tag on it and move on. Remember not to throw away the price tag, in case you decide not to buy the item and have to put the price tag back on the item.

It's important to do a thorough search of the entire house for valuable items, but not on the first pass through the house. The first pass is the time you need to find the valuable items that stick out—the obvious items that you know or think are valuable. This does not mean that you won't miss items, but you want to find as many as you can as quickly as possible. I cannot stress this point enough. You will miss some valuable items on your first pass though the house by doing such a hurried search, but you can often pick them up later. If you have missed something, then there's a good chance that others also will have missed it. What you don't want to do is miss something that is obviously valuable simply because you wasted too much time looking at other items in another part of the house.

Once I have made my way though the entire house, and I am pretty sure that I haven't missed any rooms, and I have gone through any other buildings, I start my second pass though the house. I should mention at this point that it is very important that you have not missed any areas of the house. I have completely missed rooms full of valuables, even though I was certain that I had covered every inch of the house. And I once missed an entire floor of a house until I was about ready to leave the sale. There is no simple way to guarantee this won't happen, since many older houses have many hidden doors and staircases.

You should be expeditious on your first trip through the house, moving as quickly as possible through the house and gathering up all the items that you feel are valuable. On your second pass through the house, on the other hand, you should do a thorough search.

The second pass

After you have gone quickly though all the rooms in the house and any outside buildings and gathered up all the items you think you might want to buy, you should immediately begin your second pass through the house. It is sometimes beneficial to go though the rooms in the opposite direction, or reverse order of your first trip. By going in the opposite direction, you can get a different perspective of the rooms and the items in them, which often enables you to find valuable items that you missed initially.

At times, the second pass can be more important than the first. This is when you can slow down your search somewhat and examine items more closely. However, I still conduct this second search as quickly and efficiently as possible. This is also the time that you look in corners, closets, drawers, and any other areas that you have not searched during the first pass. On my first trip through the house, I sometimes make a mental note of a closet or a dresser that I want to look at closer. For instance, if you come to an old sewing machine with a lot of drawers, you should probably pass on searching the drawers on your first trip, but rather search them quickly on your second pass through the house.

Look though drawers and closets, and examine all the items on shelves. Go through boxes. Boxes are often hidden beneath tables or furniture, and you can often find valuable items in a box that appears to contain only worthless junk. Often the family won't even price or display some of the more valuable items in boxes. You can usually find just about as many items on your second pass as you did on your first pass through the house. When I find an item on my second trip through the house, I treat it the same as if I had found it on the first trip through the house: I place the item in the box to make a final decision later.

Third pass

Once you have made it though the entire house a second time, you can begin your third and final pass. The third pass is when you should take all the time you need to search all areas of the house, including exposed crawl spaces and rafters, when they are easily accessible. I have found all kind of items that were stuck in out-of-the-way places for storage. Valuables, too, are often hidden in these areas. The third pass is when I go through clothing, records, books, and furniture. (These are the items listed in the previous chapter that I pass by on my first two trips through the house.)

If you noticed anything interesting on your first two passes, such as a stack of magazines, you might start your third search with them. Every item should be considered on your third pass through the house. Even items that you felt might not hold any value should be looked at closely and reconsidered, to make sure that you have not accidentally missed something valuable. If there are jars or containers containing buttons or other small or less valuable items, I will empty them onto a table and search through them for anything that might be valuable. I frequently find valuable items in containers packed with mostly worthless items. I have often found old coins, silver jewelry, and valuable memorabilia in these types of containers. I once found a rare pencil clip in a cardboard box filled with old pencils and crayons; I sold it for over $45. With the third pass, the policy is to search every item and every corner of the house as thoroughly as possible.

Losing your items

To reiterate, don't leave you items anywhere unattended. Even if sellers tell you that they will watch your items while you continue to shop, you should always keep your items with you. I have learned this lesson the hard way. I have, on occasion, had items removed from my containers, and once I lost a whole box of items that I had already paid for but left inside the house. Carrying your items with you can be burdensome, but it is still a good rule to follow. I don't believe that when your items are taken, it is always intentional; some buyers may believe that a box containing your items is just another box of items still up for sale, and they search the box and remove the items they want. But losing items happens frequently enough to be of real concern. It can be very frustrating to lose valuable items at this stage of the sale, when most of the hard work is finished.

Three-pass summary

Thus, my strategy at any estate sale is to make three passes through the house. The first pass should be done as quickly and efficiently as possible, seeking out obviously valuable items or items that you believe could be valuable, and collecting these items and taking them with you. The second pass is when you slow down and look at everything more thoroughly but still as efficiently as possible, opening drawers and looking inside closets and boxes. The third pass is when you can relax and make your way slowly and more deliberately through the house, looking at all areas and all objects inside the house. This is when you will look at everything. It should also be noted that most of the time, you will find a number of better items during the third pass, since many buyers will put items back that they have been carrying around and have decided not to buy.

I believe that with this simple strategy, you will succeed in buying the greatest number of valuable items possible at any estate sale. I also tend to make one final quick trip through the house after I have loaded all the items I have bought into the car. I do this because of items that others may have laid back down when they decided not to buy them, and also because things settle or get moved around enough to expose items you may have not seen initially. I also tend to examine the actual physical aspects of the house, to determine whether there might be a hidden area that I have not searched or thought to search, such as the top of a cabinet.

Types of items

The following is a list of general categories of items that you will likely encounter at almost every estate sale you attend. I have drawn up this list in the hope of simplifying the process of searching a house for valuables. I have listed the class of items and then indicated on which trip though the house I tend to look at these items. So if you find a closet full of clothes, you will know that these are items that you normally search on the last trip through the house.

1. Clothes: third pass (consider unusual or vintage clothing, leather, designer items and accessories, etc.)

2. Records: third pass (consider any albums with unusual covers or popular artists, and 45 RPM records with good picture sleeves)

3. Books: second or third pass (collect older first editions with dust jackets)

4. Furniture: third pass (any small piece of furniture with older construction, dovetailed, in excellent condition; usually pass on most furniture)

5. Glassware: first pass (cut glass, colored glass, marked, without any damage; take any items that you find with you)

6. Ceramics: first pass (marked pieces without damage)

7. Fixtures: third pass (only small, ornate, unusual fixtures; *i.e.,* switch plates, door pulls, knobs, etc.)

8. Jewelry and small items: first pass (Often these items are on the table at the front of the house, and you will be unable to take them with you. They should be looked at quickly during the first pass, and you should point out the items that you are sure you want and leave the seller your name, if you can't take them with you, and then move on quickly, paying for the items later. Look at the items more closely on your second pass. Items placed in a display case or table at the front of the house are

always a dilemma. There can be very valuable items, but you risk wasting a lot of time making the purchase. If items don't jump out at me when I pass quickly by the table, I usually wait until I have searched the rest of the house.)

9. Paper items: first pass (All paper items should be looked at during the first pass, or at least collected to be looked at the end of the third pass.)

Things not to miss

Don't forget to look at what's hanging **on the walls**—there can be valuable paintings, prints, calendars, fixtures, etc.

There are a number of items you should watch for that are located **in the garage**. First and foremost are any auto-related advertising items, particularly old metal oil cans, maps, toys, license plates, etc. On the second pass, look at smaller items in organizers for any valuable items in among the worthless items. Check for old electric items, clocks, radios, televisions, etc. Check the walls for posters and thermometers, and check under shelves.

Many older items are stored **in the basement**, and almost anything can be found there, so it's important to go though everything that's located there very carefully. Some things that are commonly missed are small bottles or cans with labels that are old, tools, and laundry items.

Don't forget to look **overhead**. Many items are placed between rafters and overhead beams and forgotten about. I have found some valuable items that the sellers were completely unaware of because they hadn't thought to look. Looking upward seems to be unnatural, even when searching a house for estate items, so when looking at items in front of you and below you, don't forget to also look at what might be overhead. Check the rafters for any items that have been put there for storage: tools, railroad items, Christmas items, etc. At a house sale some years ago, I found a rare RCA advertising sign that was being used as a shelf. Remember to be as thorough as possible.

When I am satisfied that I have covered every inch of the house and am sure that I have found all the valuable items I am likely to find, I locate a quiet place somewhere in the house where I can go through all the items I have collected, inspect them more closely, and make my final decision of what items I want to buy. I usually try to find a large, flat surface where I can lay out the items in good light, away from the traffic of other buyers.

What items do I want to keep and which ones should I put back?

Once you have finished gathering up all the items that you feel that you may want to buy and are pretty sure that you have not missed much, it's time to inspect your items more closely. The very first consideration is price. If an item is so overpriced that it is unlikely to offer a profit of at least 100 percent, I put it back. This means that if I don't think that I can get twice the price I paid for it, I will not buy the item. 100 percent profit is my absolute minimum. If the price is near my cutoff, I might consider making them an offer. But early in an estate sale, sellers are often unwilling to drop the price significantly. It is not worth risking money in buying an item that you feel might offer a profit less than twice what you will pay for it. You need at least this amount of cushion to make sure you won't lose money on the deal. If I believe the item is reasonably priced, then I will move on to the next step in deciding whether I will purchase the item. Occasionally, all of the items at an estate sale are overpriced. If this is the case, then you have to chalk it up to experience; if a professional company ran the sale, remember to stay clear of any future estate sales they may be having.

Next, I inspect each item carefully. In good light, I check all sides and surfaces, including inside surfaces, making sure the item has not been damaged or repaired. Sometimes a handle or a finial will be completely missing from an item, but it will be difficult to detect, because it detracts so little from the item, so examine each item thoroughly. Check for chips, cracks, or tears. Chips and cracks can normally be detected by running your hand across the surfaces of the item, especially around the edges of any openings. Cracks can be detected in glass items by lightly striking the mouth and listening for a clear-pitched ring. If the item is cracked, the item will give off a dull thumping sound. If you find damage, you should seriously consider not buying that item. Damaged glass or ceramic items have a significantly reduced value. Most of the time, a small chip will turn a $100 vase into a $2 vase.

Check for age. Refer to the earlier section on determining the age of an item. If it's a paper item, look for any markings, especially addresses; it should have an old-style address, one without a Zip code. Check for a phone number; if it's of any age at all, it probably will include letters or a two-, three-, or four-digit number. If it's glass, ceramic, or pottery, check for wear on the bottom; the part that comes in contact with the surface of a table should be rough with loss of the surface glaze. Check for oxidation. The surface of all items exposed to air eventually lose some of their luster though oxidation. If something is glossy or shiny, then it's most likely not that old. If you are pretty sure that the item is authentic and not some recent reproduction, and the item is not damaged, place it back into the box to buy.

I normally do not purchase items that are damaged, or in poor condition, or look like they are reproductions, or are overpriced. If you have a cell phone, you can always call someone to check the approximate value of a particular item by having them do an online search. You can also determine if the item has been heavily reproduced. However, I normally confine my calls to the more expensive items, where I am likely to lose significant amounts of money if I find out later that the item is a newer reproduction or a fantasy item.

Any item that I'm not 95 percent satisfied with, I put back. If there are postcards or magazines or other stacks of items, I examine them individually. I put back the ones that I'm not satisfied with, and if the whole group of items is for sale as one lot, then I analyze the total value of the lot. If I think that the entire lot is worth the price, than I put them all back in the box to buy. If the items collectively are not worth the price, I will sometimes separate out the items that I feel hold value and make the sellers an offer. Even then, you should keep the whole collection of items together, so that you can put them all back together as one collection if the sellers refuse your offer. Likewise, if there are a whole lot of items at one price and I'm only interested in one or two of the items, I will remove those items and make an offer to the sellers. Some sellers don't like this practice, but most of the time they will sell the separate items to you anyway.

If I have placed any tags on larger items, I first take the smaller items I have purchased to the car, and then return to evaluate the large items. As I mentioned before, I normally don't deal with larger items, because of the problems they entail. Unless I feel that an item is something that is of significant value with a very high profit potential, I will not purchase it. If, after closer inspection of the item, I determine that it is not an item I want to deal with (either because of its size or its value), I will place the price tag back on the item and remove my "sold" tag. If I do decide to buy, I make arrangements to have the item transported to my home, or occasionally I will rent a van or truck and transport the item myself. I am much more likely to purchase smaller furniture items that I can take with me at the time of the sale. Making arrangements with sellers to move items can be a major expenditure of time and effort, and can cut into your profits.

Black light

One piece of equipment that you might consider keeping handy in your car, or even carrying with you at the sale, is a black light. Black lights are very inexpensive and can come in handy at estate sales, and some are small enough that you can carry them in your coat pocket. To use one, you simply inspect the object in question under the bluish ultraviolet light. Normally this should be done in the dark or in a poorly lit area of the house. Paper manufactured after the fifties is highly fluorescent under a black light. I recommend that you become familiar with the difference between older paper and newer paper as viewed under a black light. The difference is quit dramatic, making it relatively easy to identify newer paper items. Glass, on the other hand, is just the opposite. Old glass from the fifties and before tends to give off a greenish glow under the bluish light, which is not as dramatic as paper, but still very evident. You can also detect repairs to pottery and ceramic items, because the glue and paint used for repair lights up or fluoresces under the light. Some older painted toys can be checked under black light too. Older lead-based paint colors remain consistent under the light, and there is no significant color washout, whereas newer paints tend to become muddy and dull under the light. I have been 95 percent certain something was old, only to find that I was wrong when I examined it under a black light.

Negotiate prices

Your box is full of items that you feel are of value, and you have examined them thoroughly. The next important step is to purchase your items. It's always import to attempt to negotiate prices you have to pay for your items. You can often make additional profits by negotiating lower prices for your items. However, I never make the initial offer; instead, I ask the seller if he would be willing to take anything less for the item. I have found that many times, their offer is actually less than my offer was going to be. And if they do make an offer I have established that they are willing to negotiate, and then I can make a counter-offer that is somewhat lower than their offer. If they have me make the offer, then I usually start at around 25 percent less than the item is marked, especially if it is early in the sale. Later in the sale I will usually offer about 50 percent less that the asking price. If it's a $10 item, I will normally ask the seller if he would be willing to accept $7. Many times they will say yes, and many more times they will offer a price somewhere between their original price and your offer. It is obviously better to do this with larger items, because of the larger amount of money you can actually save. And if you are buying a large number of items, the amount of money you can potentially save can be significant. Most of the time, a seller is willing to negotiate.

It is also wise to occasionally group or bundle items together, especially small lower-priced items. If you have ten smaller items with a total price of $35, you can offer the sellers less for the whole group of items. I find that sellers are normally anxious to sell as much as they can and do not want to risk losing a sale of a large number of items. If the seller offers all of the items for $30, then I will frequently make a counter-offer of a couple dollars less. But the situation has to be right, and if I have a lot of other items to buy, I tend not to get too aggressive. Most of the time, sellers are anxious to get rid of their merchandise, and in my experience they will usually accept an offer or make a counter-offers on most items.

The only other bit of advice I have about paying for your items is that you should pick your battles. In other words, you shouldn't make offers on every item you want to buy. If you start trying to get everything cheaper, sellers tend to get irritated, and sometimes they will outright tell you that they will only accept the prices that are marked on the items. Don't aggravate the sellers. Typically, if I have ten items, I will only make offers on two or three of them; this seems to be the acceptable limit. I normally wait until they have rung up four or five items before I start asking for a lower price on the next item, and I make sure that that item is one that I am likely to save the most amount of money on. Sellers are more willing to reduce their prices when they see that you are going to buy a lot of merchandise. They don't want to make you angry either.

I have frequently found that if sellers are busy when I am attempting to buy my items, in order to save time, they will just take a quick look at a few of the larger items in your container and then give you one price for the whole lot, which is typically a price significantly lower than the actual price of all the items. So occasionally I will attempt to pay for my items when the sellers are at their busiest.

Once I have paid for my items, I place them in my car. As I mentioned earlier, I make sure that the items that I want to purchase or that I have purchased are not located where some other buyer might take them, either by accident or intentionally.

Once I have placed my items in my car, I sometimes return for a final trip through the house. I do this for two reasons. The first reason is that items get moved around. Items that were initially difficult to see get moved somewhere where they can be easily seen. Also, people (like myself) tend to carry items around for a while before deciding they don't really want them and putting them back down. I am always amazed at how often I find items to buy this late in a sale, in a location I thoroughly searched less than a half-hour earlier. I also believe that I am more relaxed when the rush of the crowd is over, and I tend to be more observant. Some of my best buys have been when I returned to the house for one more quick look.

Afternoon session

Once you have thoroughly gone through the house, the only remaining question is whether you should return to the sale later, when the prices will be reduced. Most of the time, I find that it is not worth returning to a sale unless the prices were high initially. Often in this situation, few items are actually sold, and bargains can be obtained toward the end of the sale, when prices are reduced and sellers are more likely to negotiate. I have been to many estate sales where there were tons of valuable items, but they were so overpriced that no one was buying. Certain professionals routinely do this, and it's these sales that I consider returning to in the afternoon. If I see a professional service is having a sale, often I will not even attend the morning session, but rather wait until about 12:30 to go to the sale. I have found that you can often find some items worth buying at that time. The sellers are also often willing to drop the prices even lower, just to get rid of the items, especially as the end of the sale nears. I have also known buyers to carry items around for a long time in the late morning, waiting to get the item for half-price in the afternoon.

Other venues for buying valuable items

Estate sales are the best places to buy large numbers of valuable antiques, but there are other venues where you can often find reasonably priced items. At any given estate sale, you can often find thirty or forty valuable items, but at most other venues, you normally find considerably fewer items. Following are some other sites where you can often buy valuable estate items, in order of their importance.

Tag sales

Tag sales are similar to estate sales, but most of the sales are run professionally, and unfortunately the prices at tag sales are generally considerably higher than at estate sales. When I attend a tag sale, I essentially utilize the same strategy that I utilize at an estate sale. I arrive early and make three trips through the house. I find, however, that most of the time, the prices limit the number of items that I end up buying. But you can get some very good buys at tag sales, and at times you can make just as much money at a tag sale as you can at an estate sale. Tag sales should be considered high on your list of potential sales to attend, and should often be included with your list of estate sales. If an ad for a tag sale sounds better than all the estate sales advertised, that is the sale I will attend.

Flea markets

Flea markets can be a great source for reasonably priced estate-sale items. I have had some of my best days buying estate items at flea markets. Unfortunately, I have also spent hours at flea markets without finding much of anything. You normally find a lot of valuables at almost every estate sale, but at flea markets you will probably only have a good day ten to twenty percent of the time. There are times when you can find unbelievable bargains at flea markets, and if you have the time and there is a flea market near where you live, I recommend that you get up early and make the rounds. Once you get familiar with the layout, you can make the rounds rather quickly. Unlike estate sales, flea markets contain people similar to yourself who are trying to sell items they have purchased, often at the same estate sales that you have attended. The advantage is that you have a lot of sellers congregated at one location. It is important to arrive early and use the same principles that you use at estate sales to determine which items you will buy. If you see something you want, ask the seller how much they want for the item, since many items at flea markets will not be priced. When they tell you the price, make a counter-offer, if the price is reasonable. I usually offer half the asking price, which seems to be an acceptable practice. If the price is so high that it leaves no room for negotiation, just move on. And in general, if one item is overpriced, then most of the other items will be overpriced too. If I buy a large item, I have the seller hold it until I have completed my rounds.

You can also get to know some of the regular sellers at flea markets, and they will often contact you if they have any items that you might be interested in buying. Over the years, I have dealt with a few flea-market regulars and have gotten some excellent buys. I normally pass out my cards liberally to the dealers at flea markets in the area.

I cannot highly recommend flea markets as a source of large quantities of estate-sale items, but it is enjoyable just to walk around on a nice morning and shop for valuable items and occasionally make some excellent buys. At flea markets, you also have people selling newer merchandise, and you can sometimes find fantastic bargains on newer items. I once bought thousands of dollars' worth of new, high-quality amber jewelry at about one-tenth its actual value, from a store owner who had gone out of business.

Auctions

Most of the time, I have been relatively disappointed with auctions. Auctions tend to bring out the dealers and the specialized collectors, both of which are difficult to compete with. They will probably know more about most of the items then you will. It is wise to stay out of a bidding war with someone who knows a lot more about an item than you do. Many collectors are fanatics who possess unbelievable knowledge about their field of collecting. There are a number of exceptions, though, and you can get good buys at auctions. I especially like on-site auctions, since they always seem to have a number of unadvertised items, and they are often less heavily attended. On-site auctions are auctions that are held at the home where the items to be sold are located, as opposed to an auction that is held at an actual auction house. At an on-site auction, I recently made an exceptional buy on a number of toys, still in their original packaging. I believe that I got such a good buy because these items were not mentioned in the newspaper ad for the sale. If the items had been advertised, there likely would have been many toy collectors and dealers present, who would have pushed the bid price much higher. On-site auctions also seem to contain much more ephemera (old paper items, cans, bottles, etc.), which can be very valuable, but are very seldom advertised.

My strategy at an auction is to arrive as early as possible, so that I can inspect all the merchandise that will be auctioned. I especially inspect all the box lots. These are items that have been lumped together for sale in lots because, according to the auctioneers, the items are not valuable enough to sell separately. But in reality, the reason auctioneers lump items together is usually to save time. You should look at all the items in the boxes and note any boxes that contain potentially valuable items. I always write items I am interested in on the back of my bid card, along with the price I'm willing to pay. I also note the location and description of the box, since at times it is difficult to identify which box lot is actually being auctioned. Also, you can often get a good buy on an item that the other bidders have overlooked or are unaware of its true value. However, this is a relatively rare occurrence at most auctions today, since there are usually many educated and suave bidders in attendance.

At an auction, you also have the time to research any item you may be interested in buying. You can use your cell phone to call someone who has access to the Internet and have them do an online search on an item. I was at an auction recently where an oil sign was being sold as an authentic sign dating from the forties. There was considerable interest from a number of bidders, but the sign didn't appear authentic to me, because it was an item from the forties being auctioned with items that were mostly from the sixties and seventies. I made a call to a friend and had him do an online search for the sign, and he was able to determine that it was a reproduction item from the late eighties. The sign, with an actual value of about $20, sold for $360. Obviously there were a number of buyers who mistakenly believed it to be authentic. The opposite is also true, and you can often make a good buy on an item that is more valuable than the other bidders believe by taking the time to have someone do an online search for you.

With auctions, I set a strict upper limit of what I feel is an acceptable bid price, and almost never exceed that price. I try not to get emotionally attached to any item. I believe that at auctions, there is always a lot of emotional bidding. People see an item and are convinced they have to have it at any cost, for one reason or another, or believe that it is actually worth a lot more than it is. The bidding can get out of control quickly. I have literally seen a winning bidder trying to sell an item to the back bidder shortly after the bidding ended—for less than he paid—after realizing he probably paid too much for it.

I usually can judge an auction by the first half-hour. If most items are selling for reasonable prices, then I stay. If most items are bringing more than their real value, I leave. It's basically a waste of time to wait around to bid on items that will, more than likely, go for an unacceptably high price.

But to reiterate, I find auctions to be a relatively poor source of items that I can resell for a profit, and so auctions are somewhat low on my list of places to buy valuable antiques. I should state, however, that as you get more familiar with collectibles and valuable items, it becomes easier to identify good buys at auctions. The more auctions you attend, the better you get at judging value. Auctions can be exciting and very fun to attend, and occasionally you can make some great buys.

Online auctions

Surprisingly, you can often make some excellent buys online. I am never really sure why a certain item at a certain time sells for a lot less than its value, considering all the bidders that use online auctions, but you can occasionally get some excellent buys online. The profit you will make if you resell an item that you've purchased online is usually less than items bought at estate sales, but you can normally find items that, when relisted (or held for a short time and then relisted), will bring a 50 percent to 100 percent profit. You are also buying an item that comes already packaged, if you decide to sell it later.

My strategy for buying online is a strategy many buyers are very familiar with, called "sniping." In short, this is waiting until the last minute of an auction to place a bid on an item that you feel is a good buy. The bid should be one that you feel will allow you to make a profit, and not any higher. Occasionally you will get an item for a bargain price, but most of the time there will be other bidders like yourself watching the item closely, who will also place a bid in the last minute of the sale. There are computer programs that will place the bid for you while you are away from your computer. I have also found a strategy that is just the opposite of late bidding: early bidding on "buy it now" items that have just been listed. I go to the "just listed" section of the auction site and find the items that are marked "buy it now." This way, you can buy an item before it's viewed by a lot of potential bidders. I have gotten some excellent buys using this strategy. Ultimately, though, bidding online comes down to what you feel the item is worth, and in reality, this may be the best strategy. Leave your maximum acceptable bid on the item you are interested in buying, and then just forget about it. If you win the item, great! If you don't win the item, then at least you know that you didn't get emotionally involved in the bidding and pay too much

Garage sales, basement sales, and yard sales

I tend to stay away from garage sales and similar types of sales. You will occasionally see one advertised as the "first garage sale ever" after fifty years of collecting, or something similar. Sometimes, when time permits, I will stop at these sales. I have had some luck at garage sales over the years, but I very seldom attend garage sales these days. Most of the time, it's families trying to get rid of their junk or newer items they no longer have room for, and there are typically few older quality items to be found. It's also just too inefficient. There are too many garage sales to try to determine which ones are the best, and normally by the time you get to them, most of the good items have already been sold. There are just too many times you will come away empty-handed.

Advertising

You can often obtain valuable items through advertising. There are a lot of places where you can advertise for free, such as trade papers and online sites, but you can also have cards printed that state you are interested in buying estate items. Occasionally you will learn about estate sales or items that people are trying to sell by handing out your cards. It can be a golden opportunity to learn about estate sales, especially if you learn about them before everyone else. I have, on occasion, been able to search a house for items before the estate sale was even advertised.

Antique malls or co-ops

I also occasionally buy items at an antique store, usually an antique co-op or mall. Antique malls and co-ops are antique stores where spaces are rented to many dealers and collectors to sell their items. It is unusual not to find items at antique stores that are significantly underpriced. Items at co-ops are often misidentified and therefore underpriced, offering the possibility of an excellent buy. But always be aware of the possibility that the item might actually be a reproduction or a fantasy item. Reproductions and fantasy items are frequently sold at antique co-ops and antique malls.

Salvation Army or Goodwill-type stores

Some years ago, it was possible to find items at Salvation Army and Goodwill stores, but these venues seem to have pretty much dried up as a source of valuable items. Mostly this is due to the fact that the stores are now on the lookout for valuable items that have been donated. Now most stores have individuals whose main job is to look for and sell these items online. Six or seven years ago, I bought hundreds of sterling-silver charms from the sixties and seventies that had been donated by a store that had gone out of business. Most of them were valued at between $5 and $10, but I bought them all for 25¢ each. Those days have virtually ended, though.

Salvage yards

Most of the items you will find at salvage yards or junkyards are larger architectural items that are usually too large to consider buying, but occasionally you will find smaller antiques that the owners of the salvage yard have found when demolishing a structure. Sometimes they are involved in tearing down houses or businesses, and they bring in items that were left behind at the house. I have made arrangements with a worker at one salvage yard to call when any older items are brought in for resale. I recently purchased an old television for $20 and sold it for just under $250.

Resale shops and consignment stores

You can frequently find items at resale shops and consignment stores, but the yield is too low to consider shopping at them often. I will usually only go through these stores a couple times a year, but I occasionally find some valuable items to resell. I should mention that it is of value to find someone on the inside at these sites to keep you informed about any items you may be interested in buying. It is difficult and time-consuming to keep watch on a number of different sites, especially when the chance of finding a significant number of items is low. But if you can make arrangements with someone at the store to notify you when any older items are brought in, then the site can become a very important source of valuable antique items. I normally give a finder's fee for anything that I end up buying.

Now that you have purchased your items, you can begin the process of reselling your items. In the following chapter, I will outline how this can be done and tell you where you can sell your items for the highest profit.

5

Selling Your Valuable Items

There are a number of different venues that I normally use to sell the valuable items I have acquired at estate sales and at other sites. However, I sell most of my items at just one place: eBay. This is an online auction service for buying and selling items over the Internet; most readers are probably already familiar with it. You can easily access eBay's Web site, and the instructions on how to use the service are very simple to follow. One of the greatest advantages of selling an item online is that you are exposing that particular item to millions of potential bidders. This is one of the primary reasons that the buying and selling of estate items has become profitable. Items that were difficult to sell in the past now can be sold rather easily through eBay or similar online sites.

I almost exclusively sell my more valuable items online through eBay, but I often use other sites to sell my less valuable items, especially any items I feel are worth less than about $10. The cost and effort to list an item of this smaller value outweighs the small profit you will likely make. I sell these items elsewhere, at locations that I will discuss later. I do, however, group similar items like postcards or small toys together to sell online, to increase the overall value of the listing. Over the years, I have developed some of my own strategies for selling estate items online. My strategy—or, for that matter, everyone's basic strategy—is to present the item to the potential bidders in such a way that you will achieve the highest sale price. The following is the general procedure that I follow. Along the way, I will point out some important facts that may be helpful in attaining the maximum prices for your items.

Writing out the description of the item to be sold

The first and most important step to take when preparing your item to sell online is to write out a detailed description of the item. It is important to understand some basic principles about selling on eBay. To get as many bidders as possible, you must utilize the tools available to attract them, and that starts with the description of the item. This is important, since this is the way that potential bidders will be drawn to your item. EBay is designed so that a bidder can use any word in your description to find your item. Thus, your description should be as detailed and comprehensive as possible. This means that you should list anything and everything that you know or can find out about the item. This description should not only include important details about the item; you should also include information about the item that you feel may not be all that important.

Let's assume you are attempting to sell an RCA Bakelite radio. If a potential bidder on eBay types in the word "radio," you will get bidders, but if your description includes "RCA," you will get more potential bidders, and if it includes "Bakelite," you will get even more potential bidders. This is the basic principle behind listing as much information about an item as you can.

It is imperative to list any buzzword in your description to attract bidders. Buzzwords are words that buyers often use to search for a particular item. I have seen many items on eBay sell for considerably less than their actual value because their descriptions were poor. The following is a general list of aspects of an item that should be included when listing it on eBay.

1. Describe the materials the item is made of, and any manufacturing processes that were involved in making the item. Materials such as Bakelite, celluloid, or Lucite should always be listed, since there are collectors who specialize in items because they are made of a particular material. If it's plastic, make sure that you describe it as either hard plastic or soft plastic. Hard plastic tends to mean an older item. It is also important to list anything you might know about the manufacturing processes. Tin litho, cut glass, or keywound—list anything that places the item into a special group of like items. Also, note the colors of the item.

2. List any markings that are found on the item. This can be the most important part of your description. You should list maker's marks, dates, patent numbers, addresses, etc. Describe any markings you find, or include photographs of them.

3. List anything you know about the item. If you have identified the maker, make sure you include that in your description. There are many collectors who specialize in just one particular maker, and some of these items can bring a premium. It is also important to list the town and state where it was manufactured. Some people collect by region of the country. Also, list anyone who may be associated with an item, such as who actually designed the item or signed the item, and include any history about them that you know.

If you think a vase might be a piece of Fenton glass even though it is not marked, it is important to state your impressions. Fenton collectors will be able to find the item, and then they can decide if the item is a Fenton. If they are serious collectors, they will know if it is or isn't, and if they don't, they will contact you with their questions. Make sure you make every attempt to assure them that you know what you have. I once bought a tray of small items at an estate sale, and later was approached by an older individual who told me that the container the items were in was worth more than the items themselves. It was a Fry pie plate. I didn't know a thing about the Fry company, and I probably would have discarded the pie plate or sold it for a lot less than it was actually worth. A glass pie plate is almost worthless, but a Fry plate can be worth close to fifty dollars. The point is that most of the time, you should know what you are buying and selling. Attempt to identify all items before you try to sell them. It could mean the difference between a small profit and a very large profit.

4. Describe where you found the item. "Bought at an older estate sale" usually suffices, but you can list other information about the estate sale that you think might help. Tell about the owner, if it's relevant. If you bought a Campbell Soup advertising item, it would be important to tell the potential bidders if the owner happened to be an employee of Campbell Soup Company; it lends authenticity to the item. Sometimes telling the bidders that you are selling other items from the estate lends credibility to your item, and this can often lead potential bidders to look at the other items you have up for sale.

5. List any damage. If there are any tears, breaks, cracks, chips, crazing, wear, etc., it should all be listed. The size and location of the damage should be described: "a 5mm by 8mm chip on the rim," "a 1cm tear," etc. It is important to list any flaws or damage, even if it is minor, to insure that the buyer is well aware of any problems with the item. If the damage doesn't detract from the appearance of the item, I will state that in my description. You don't want to have to go through the trouble of having the item returned if the buyer informs you that he was unaware of the damage. You will have lost time and money, and your item will still be unsold.

6. At the end of your description, always give all the dimensions, colors, and weight of the item, especially when weight and size will be a consideration with postage.

A typical description of an item might be:

> McCoy cookie jar, clown in barrel, Mold #40, marked "McCoy USA" along two lines at base, made at Zanesville Ohio Plant around 1950, colors very bright with no chips but very small hairline crack at base, pictured, approximately ½ inch. Found at older estate sale with many other antique items that I am selling. Lists for $150 in 1994 edition of Wilson's *Antique Values*. 11 1/2 inches high, 3 lbs., 4 oz. Rare item in excellent condition.

To reiterate, it is important to know what you're selling. Do your research. You can do this online though eBay or at other online sites, or get information from a dealer you trust. You could be missing a very valuable item, so do whatever it takes to identify an item, especially something that you feel might be of particular value.

I recently bought the head of a Dutch girl made out of plaster at an estate sale for 50¢. After I paid for it, the seller jokingly told me that she didn't know what the hole in the mouth was. When I told her that the item was a string holder and that the mouth was where the string came out, she was disappointed. She knew that string holders were valuable, but she hadn't realized what she was selling. If you have an item that is improperly identified and listed that way online, you risk losing a considerable amount of money.

Here is a good example to demonstrate how misidentifying an item can mean you receive less money. A pie bird, like the name suggests, is a small ceramic figure in the shape of a bird that was typically used in the forties and fifties when baking pies. The pie bird was place on top of the pie in such as way as to release steam from beneath the crust. These pie birds were usually colorful, and they depicted various species of birds. Some pie birds are very collectible and very valuable. To list this item simply as "a colorful ceramic bird" would most likely bring bids considerably less than if it was listed properly as a pie bird. The point I'm trying to convey is that this is common mistake sellers make, and it extends across all fields of collecting. Some rare misidentified items can be almost worthless unless they are properly identified.

I also do a search on eBay of any like items. EBay offers this service through a "complete listings" prompt under the search option, which gives you information on similar items that have sold. It gives you prices and information concerning the item that can be very helpful in writing your description. It also gives you buzzwords that might be beneficial to use in your description. It is also good to determine how many similar items are being sold at the time you plan to list your item. If there are any more than two similar items, then I will wait for a better opportunity to list the item. You don't want to be in competition with other sellers of the same item. If multiple items are sold at the same time, it tends to hold down the prices. If you are the only one listed, you have a better chance of receiving a higher final bid.

The next step I take is to photograph the item. Once you have drawn in bidders with your detailed description, you can often pique their interest with the photographs you provide. A picture can be taken, scanned, and uploaded to eBay, but it is much easier to use a digital camera, where the images can be directly transferred onto the online site. The transferred images are normally of better quality than a scanned photograph. I normally take two photos, front and back, unless it is a particularly valuable item. Then I will take up to six photos, showing each side of the object. I usually do this under good direct light without the flash, and at a camera setting designed for close-up photography. Flash photography usually causes shadows that can distort the appearance of an item. I attempt to photograph the item at angles, and not at direct-on views. I also photograph any markings on the object and any damaged areas. The first photo can be added without any additional charge for the listing. Make sure that the pictures are of the best quality possible. If they're not and the item is at all blurry or difficult to see, it appears that you are trying to hide something, and you will typically lose a lot of potential bidders. This is another good reason to use a digital camera, since you can take and view multiple photos before choosing the ones you are satisfied with. I have seen some sellers show items in an attic or basement, surrounded by other antiques, giving the impression that it is old or has been stored there for a long time. I think that this practice is a subtle form of deception, but I also believe that it does pique the interest of many potential bidders.

The question always arises of whether you should clean or make minor repairs before you photograph the object to be sold; I would say no in most situations. Collectors like to buy items in their original found condition (the actual condition in which they were found), believing that it adds to the authenticity of an item if it is dusty and dirty. I tend to agree with this, unless it absolutely detracts significantly from the item. If photographs give the impression that an item is of a significantly lower grade than it actually is, you should probably clean the item very carefully, and only if the complete integrity of the item can be maintained. The layer of dust often found on older paper items can be wiped with a soft, dry cloth, but no further cleaning attempts should be made. Attempts at removing dirt and stains can damage the surface of an item if not done properly. If you damage an item, you can significantly reduce its value. If it is truly a valuable paper item and you feel that cleaning would add significantly to the value, then you should take it to a documents conservator, who can determine whether the document can be restored and tell you how much it will cost. The same principle holds with other items. Grease and dirt can usually be removed from the surface of metal and glass items with a damp cloth, but avoid vigorous attempts at removing stains, especially from metal items. Vigorous attempts at removing a stain by rubbing can cause the loss of paint and a dulling of the surface. If you feel that it will greatly increase the value of an item, then you should consider restoration. Personally, I find that the amount of time and effort in most situations does not warrant professional restoration. I usually leave that up to the buyer, and as I already mentioned, many buyers are much more satisfied buying an item that is in the original condition in which it was found instead of an item that has been restored. Part of many collectors' joy in collecting is restoring the objects that they buy.

Some of the more important factors to consider when listing an item on eBay are as follows:

1. Once you are satisfied with the description, you should determine the category under which you will list your item on eBay. Most experienced bidders will do a general search and find most items, but some items might be better listed under more than one category. For example, if you are trying to sell an antique woman's watch, you could conceivably list the item under at least three different categories. The most likely place to list it would be under "jewelry and watches," but you might also list it in the "antiques" category, and it could also be listed under "collectibles." It is important to determine which of the categories might be the most successful at bringing the highest price. This is one of the reasons it's important to describe the watch as an "antique woman's watch." That way, a general search will likely locate the watch regardless of which category it is listed under. There's no reason that it can't be listed under more than one category, but it is more expensive, and most experienced eBay buyers will do a general search to find the items that they are interested in finding. I often find that if the item is of significant value, it is beneficial to list it under more than one category or as a featured item. It is more expensive to have the item listed as a premier or featured item, but it attracts significantly more attention to the item and tends to generate more potential bidders and a higher winning bid. When you listed it as a featured item, it will appear at the top of the list of all the other items, and it will be one of the first items potential bidders see.

2. Next, determine a minimum bid or a reserve price. This is usually the minimum amount that I will accept for the item. I normally determine this by taking the price I have paid for the item and factoring in a reasonable profit. In most cases, I start with no reserve or a very small minimum opening bid. I have arguments for and against not having a reserve, but I personally I feel that you get more interest if you start your items out low. You can get people excited about an item if they think they will be able to get the item at a very low price. Bidders will continue to watch the item, and they may bid the item to a much higher price than they normally would have if there had been a higher reserve. I also think that a reserve sometimes prevents people from bidding. Even if the reserve price is reasonable, some bidders are less likely to bid, or will watch the item to bid on it later. There are other options when listing an item, such as "buy it now," but I believe that most of these options limit the overall profits you will make selling items on eBay.

3. Next, weigh the item and list the price of shipping and handling. Actual charges by Zip code area can be listed as a payment option; this is available through eBay's shipping calculator. I usually only charge a minimal amount for the materials and handling—usually close to my actual cost. Items seem to sell better when people are not initially burdened with a large handling charge.

4. You also need to choose the type of payment you will accept. This is a personal preference, but because the number of items that I sell is limited, I tend to accept all forms of payment other than credit card. The paperwork and cost to set up credit-card payment is somewhat burdensome. PayPal is an option that eBay offers; you can get your items paid for immediately if the buyer has a PayPal account.

Packaging and shipping your items

Package each item securely with adequate packing material, especially fragile items. I send most items through the United States Postal Service, but you can set up an account with UPS or FedEx to handle your shipping. These services can make the shipping and handling of your items a lot easier. They supply boxes, and you can print shipping labels and postage from your computer and then arrange to have them pick up your items at your house. Stamps.com is a site where postage can be obtained online for a small fee. Often you can obtain used boxes and packing material from local businesses without charge, but this is somewhat inconvenient, and most of the time I prefer to ship my items in standard-sized boxes. Standard-sized boxes are usually much easier to handle. You should offer insurance and request a delivery confirmation for any valuable items, to prevent any claim that your package never arrived. The United States Postal Service offers delivery confirmation without charge when done online.

I tend to wait until I have at least thirty or forty items to list. I photograph them all and then go through the process of listing each one. Although there are varying opinions on the best time to list an item, I tend to list my items on Saturday or Sunday between 3:00 PM and 9:00 PM Eastern Standard Time. I list them for seven-day auctions, so that the bidding will end at the same time the following week. I believe these times are the best hours to attract the most number of bidders at the most important time of the auction. Unfortunately, weekends are also the time when the bidding on most items ends. This can detract from the sale of your items if there are too many items ending at the same time. So I often list my items on other days of the week. Some studies have found that Thursday is the best day to end an auction, but I have not noticed a large difference, and occasionally you will find that an item that ends late at night will bring a better price than one listed at other times. A strategy that some bidders use is to look for items that end at strange hours, such at 2:00 or 3:00 AM, believing that there will be fewer bidders at this hour of the day. It can work at times, but in my experience, the ending bids are usually just about as high (if not higher) than the bids on similar items ending at a better time of the day.

Once the auction has ended, eBay notifies the winning bidder with their winning bid and shipping information. I also e-mail the winning bidder with the exact charges, and then wait for payment. Once payment is made and verified, I package and ship the merchandise.

If I have a non-payer, which happens occasionally, I will e-mail the buyer, and if I still get no response, I will file a complaint with eBay and leave negative feedback on the bidder's site. I find that it is not worth the time and effort to try to get my money when a bidder refuses to pay. As a seller, you're only out your time and the amount of money you spent listing the item. You can always relist and sell your item later, or contact the back bidder, if you want. If an item fails to get any bids, I will wait at least three months before I relist it, although there's no reason why you can't list it immediately. If it doesn't sell after a second listing, then I will sell the item at a different site. If I see that there is very little interest in the item, by checking the number of bidders that actually looked at the item, then I will also sell it at a different site. It is important to put a reserve price on any higher-priced items. If you have paid $50 for an item, then you should probably set a reserve price of at least $75. You do not want to lose money by selling the item for less than you paid for it, and this can happen occasionally.

When selling on an online site like eBay, it is important to learn all the options available to sell your items, and this usually comes with time. It can initially be somewhat complicated, but once you become familiar with the site, the whole process of selling becomes much easier, and you will be able to determine which options work best for you.

I also believe that there are a number of other venues where you can sell the items that you have purchased at estate sales and other sites, which I will discuss below.

Antique stores, malls, or co-ops

I have found that antique co-ops can be very good places to sell my lower-priced items and selected higher-priced items. Antique co-ops are antique stores that rent spaces or booths to individual antique dealers; you can find them in almost any town. Co-ops can be a very convenient and efficient way to sell your estate items, and in many ways it is much easier than selling your items online. For starters, you don't have to go through the work of listing, packaging, and shipping the items. I usually sell small items with limited value that are probably not worth the cost of selling at an online auction site. Co-ops normally have spaces of different sizes and prices. They normally also have locked display cases, which prevents your items from being stolen or accidentally moved to another dealer's booth. I make sure that I mark all my items clearly with the name of the item and the price, so that it can be seen without the case being opened. I also make sure that my booth or space number is listed on the tag.

Co-ops and malls usually charge by the month, the charge depending on the size of the rented space. The usual charges range from about $10 to $50 a mouth. I own my own small locked display case, where I place many of my smaller items. This saves the money of renting one of the store's display cases. I normally place all my larger items near the case. Antique co-ops are a way to sell some of your lower-priced merchandise and also some larger items that are difficult to ship. You can also have more control over your prices. I normally start my price high and then continue to drop the price until the item is sold. On one case, I list items and state that the items are reduced by 10 percent a week; this brings back buyers who are waiting for the item to drop to a level they find acceptable. (Buyers occasionally will pay the higher price, fearing that an item might be sold to someone else if they wait too long.) I also make sure that I am easily accessible by cell phone, so that the workers at the co-op can call me with any offers on my items at any time. If the price of an item gets too low, I usually remove the item and try again later, or attempt to sell it at a different venue.

I also like co-ops because they allow you to advertise. I put up a sign in my display case that states that I am interested in buying any estate items and antiques, and leave cards on top of the display case. Whether to pass out business cards is a personal preference, but I find that it can be very beneficial. I have gotten many leads and have made some excellent buys from people who have contacted me after seeing one of my cards. I highly recommend that you have business cards printed and pass them out liberally. I list my phone number and e-mail address and state that I am interested in buying estate items, entire estates, and any item forty years old or older.

I usually state on the card that I am interested in one piece or the whole estate, but in reality I very seldom consider buying an entire estate. Stating that I buy entire estates does occasionally afford me the opportunity to inspect an entire estate and to make offers on items that I am interested in buying. I have spent weeks going though estates, searching for valuable items to buy. Obtaining the ability to search a house for valuable items is a golden opportunity, and you can often make thousand of dollars in profit. To buy an entire estate instead of selected objects, however, means that you will have to dispose of many larger items and items that have little value. This task can be a difficult and unprofitable proposition, and the time and money necessary to conduct an actual estate sale can also be difficult and a lot less profitable than cherry-picking the most valuable items from the estate. It is much more profitable to only deal with the more valuable items of an estate.

After I am done placing my items in my rental space, I take time to look over other dealers' items. As I mentioned earlier, I frequently find items that are underpriced or misidentified.

Auctions

Occasionally I will sell some of my items at auction. The prices achieved at auctions can often be unpredictable; however, most of the time you will receive a lower bid than you would have received at an online auction. The obvious reason for this is that there are just fewer bidders bidding on your items. On the other hand, it is somewhat easier to sell items at an auction than online. You can simply gather up the items that you haven't been able to sell online or at your co-op and take them to the auction. Occasionally you will actually get higher bids at auction than you will online. I have had items that have failed to sell online, but at auction, they did just fine.

I usually accumulate a good number of items before I take them to auction, instead of taking one or two items at a time. I make sure that the auctioneer is familiar with the items I am selling, and inform him of any significant facts about the item (maker, age, etc.). Along with items that I have been unsuccessful in selling at other sites, I also sell items at auctions that are not in the best of condition. That way, potential bidders can actually examine the items before they bid. Often when you sell damaged items on eBay, buyers will send them back, even if you have accurately described their condition problems. Sometimes even a small defect in an item is an excuse for a buyer to send an item back to you. This becomes a problem, and you can end up wasting a lot of time, effort, and money absorbing the cost of the failed sale and the cost of attempting to resell your item. I also tend to sell locally related items at local auctions. These items tend to sell better when they have some connections to the region and to the potential bidders. There are usually many avid collectors of local material in any given community, who often bid aggressively against each other, pushing prices higher.

When selling items at an auction, you have to take into consideration the commission that the auction is going to charge to sell your items. Most of the time, it is about 25 percent. There are a few auctioneers who will balk at selling a small number of items, but most auctioneers will sell your items regardless of their value or the number of items that you have to sell. It is probably best to pick one auctioneer that you can trust and feel comfortable working with.

Flea markets

About once a year, I go to a local flea market and sell the items that I have been unable to sell throughout the year. Most of these items are my mistakes, items that I probably shouldn't have purchased. Most of them are items that I failed to properly identify, or that I identified correctly but overestimated their value or collectibility—usually reproductions, fantasy items, or damaged items. Most of the time, you will make only a small profit or even actually lose a small amount of money on these items. I usually like to take them to a well-known flea-market site to ensure that there will be a large number of people looking at the items. At this point in trying to sell an item, I will seriously consider any offer I receive, as I am attempting to sell all the items that I have brought to the flea market. At this point, a small loss on items is acceptable, and you can at least get some of your money back on the mistakes you bought.

I also look at the "wanted to buy" ads. I have sold and bought items this way, but it is a very small percentage of my business.

Natural progression of selling your items

A word concerning the buying and selling of valuable items and antiques. I believe that in general, the venues for selling your items should follow a natural progression. Any item that you have purchased, regardless of where, should initially be attempted to be sold at an online auction site. If the item doesn't sell online, then you should attempt to sell it at an antique shop, then at auction, and finally at a flea market. The money you receive tends to decrease consistently depending on where the item is sold; you will usually receive the lowest price at a flea market and the highest price at an online auction. Even when you buy an item at a flea market, you should use this progression and attempt to sell the item first at an online site. I see too many dealers who buy items at auctions and then try to sell the items at flea markets. Sometimes they are successful, but more often they are stuck with items they can't sell for the price they paid for them. I have often bought items at flea markets for less than what I know the seller paid for them at auction.

6

Rules of the Game

Important things to remember at estate sales

1. Find the right estate sale. Make sure that the estate sale you attend is the sale with the most potential of having valuable estate items.

2. Take with you (a) detailed instructions to the site of the sale, (b) a medium-sized container for your items, and (c) enough money to pay for your items.

3. Arrive early—the earlier, the better.

4. Be thorough and efficient in your search of the house. Search every nook and cranny and every box, drawer, and closet. Don't miss anything. You will find valuable items in all parts of the house.

Remember, the most important time of an estate sale is the first hour. Most valuable items at any estate sale are purchased during the first hour.

Make three passes through the house

1. On the first trip, you should quickly move though the house, collecting items that you believe are valuable. Don't spend a lot of time looking or deciding which items you want; just take the items and put them in your container. Decide later what you really want to buy.

2. You should be more thorough during your second pass through the house, looking at everything in all areas of the house as quickly and efficiently as you can, trying not to miss anything. This is when you open drawers and closet doors and look through boxes—but do so as quickly and efficiently as possible.

3. The third trip though the house is when you look at certain items you didn't look at closely enough during the first two trips though the

house: books, magazines, clothes, fixtures, stained-glass windows, tile, etc. You should go over every inch of the house thoroughly and at a relaxed pace.

4. Consider a fourth trip through the house once you have paid for your items and have placed them safely in your car, especially if the estate is a large one located in a large house with many rooms. This is when you can often find items that others have decided they didn't want and put back down, or items that were not initially evident but have been exposed by other buyers moving objects around.

Make sure that you did not miss looking at any rooms in the house altogether. This can occur very easily if you aren't careful. Make sure that you have not missed any buildings outside the main house, such as garages and storage sheds. You can often find many valuable items in these locations.

After your third pass through the house, inspect each item before you decide to buy it

1. Check each item separately, initially checking for any damage to the item. Make sure the item is complete and has no missing parts. Make sure that it is not just part of a set; you don't want to buy a salt shaker without the matching pepper shaker. Check the quality of the item, especially jewelry. Examine items for any markings.

2. Attempt to determine if it is authentic. Look for any marks identifying it as a reproduction. Look for damage that may have been intentionally made to hide the fact that it is a newer reproduction. Use a black light if necessary. Most of the time, this is not necessary. Most items at estate sales are period items, but there are occasions when you should check your items.

3. Make sure the price is low enough that you are pretty sure that you will make a substantial profit when you sell it.

4. Put back any items that you are not satisfied with, including those that are broken, damaged, or that you feel are likely to be reproductions. (If they are cheap enough, it might be worth taking the chance, if you're not sure.) Call a friend with any questions that you have about any more expensive items.

Negotiate prices with the seller, but do so tactfully. If possible let the seller make the first offer, but if not, always make a reasonable offer. Chose your battles wisely.

After you have purchased your items, take them to your car. Don't leave them inside the house or in the care of anyone else, especially the sellers. Some other buyer is likely to go through your boxes if they are left unattended, and sellers are often too busy to watch everyone's items. You definitely don't want to lose a valuable item at this point in the sale.

Factors that will help you maximize your profits at estate sales

1. Know what you want to buy. Know what people are collecting—glassware, advertising, toys, etc. There are books that list the items most commonly collected. Buy one and look at it frequently to become familiar with these classes of items. A good source is the *Flea Market Price Guide,* which is loaded with hundreds of categories of collectables. Know which items are hot. Pay particular attention to newer items that are still in their original packaging.

2. Learn to judge the age and authenticity of an item, to avoid buying items that are newer reproductions. The more estate sales you attend, the easier it becomes to evaluate the authenticity and value of your items. The important things to check for are as follows:

   a. Check for wear on the surfaces of the item that come in contact with other objects or surfaces; *e.g.,* handles and the bases of older items should show wear from use.

   b. Check for oxidation; this is the dulling of most surfaces. If it looks new and shiny, it probably is. Most older items have dull surfaces.

   c. Check for normal signs of aging: foxing, crazing, etc.

   d. Remember tags, stickers, and marks can be added to anything, and reproduction labels can also be removed. Lift stickers and check for any discoloration that might indicate the sticker has been there for some time.

   e. Beware if it is an item that can easily be reproduced, like just about any paper item. Beware even more if the item is easily reproducible and is a popular brand, like Coca-Cola. It is very likely a reproduction. As they say, "If it's too good to be true, it probably is!"

f. Watch for "salting," the very common practice of bringing newer items into an estate sale to sell them as part of an older estate. The real problem with salting is that it lends credibility to newer reproduction items just by the fact that they are being sold in the company of older estate items. Remember, if you find one, there could be many.

3. Try to be a generalist. You should know a little bit about as much as possible. You have to be able to judge all the items at an estate sale for their potential worth, not just a few specific classes of items. This ability increases your likelihood of finding the most valuable items. If you find a piece of pottery, you can't be expected to always identify its value or maker in the field, but you can learn to recognize quality and know that if it bears a maker's mark, then it will likely have value. You can always identify the maker and value later.

4. Use a black light if you're not sure if the item is old or authentic. It is the one tool you can take with you that can help you verify the authenticity of an item. You will be surprised at how often an older-looking item will actually be newer. Check the edges of paper. Check for repairs. Check glass. Check even when you get your items to the car, and if an item isn't old, return it to the seller. New paper and old glass fluoresces, as do areas of an item that have been repaired.

5. Remember the "thirty-year rule." Items that are around thirty years old are generally more valuable than older items, since many collectors are reaching for items they had when they were young. The opposite can also happen: older items can actually get less valuable because there are fewer collectors searching for those items.

6. Build a reference library of books that will help with identification of the items that you buy, such as *Lehner's Encyclopedia of US Marks*. I always find it helpful to browse through the collectible and antique section of larger bookstores, such as Barnes and Noble. They normally have a great selection of books dealing with antiques. I generally stay away from books that attempt to cover many areas of collecting, and focus more on the books that give information about a specific area of collecting.

7. Always be learning. Talk to other collectors and buyers. They are a wealth of information, and information is very helpful in this business.

What you learn from others can turn into profits later. But remember, advice from a dealer interested in buying your items is not always reliable. In that situation, I will do my own research or get advice elsewhere. When you buy an item, don't just research the item; research the whole class of items. Every item you buy is a lesson you can learn and use at your next estate sale. Identifying and researching your purchases can be an enjoyable pastime that can add to your profits.

8. Let people know that you are interested in attending estate sales and buying estate items. Have business cards printed and pass them out liberally. Talk to professionals that hold estate sales and tell them that you would like to attend any pre-sales they might be having. Advertise in newspapers or trade papers. Do anything you can to make people aware of your interest in estate sales.

9. Make estate sales a game. The more you understand the rules and the more you play, the better you will become and the more money you will make.

10. Learn your lessons well. I learn something almost every week. Sometimes someone will educate you, and sometimes you will discover things by yourself. There are thousands of tricks to the trade. My latest revelation occurred about three months ago. When I was young, I collected coins, but it was never a serious hobby, and I certainly was never interested in collecting foreign coins. I went to an estate sale, where I found a group of Canadian coins in an old tin container. I normally look at all coins to make sure that there are no US coins among them that have gone unrecognized by the seller; this happens quite frequently. But when I looked, I found that most of them were in excellent condition, and one silver nickel from 1905 looked as if it was in uncirculated condition. I paid $5 for all of the coins, and eventually sold all of them for about $300. After all these years, I had learned something new. Canadian coins in this country were brought back by the thousands and thrown in boxes and cupboards and forgotten about. Canadian coins found in the United States are generally in better condition, and can be worth a lot more money for that reason alone. I had been violating one of my rules by not looking more closely at coins. I wondered how many similar coins I had passed over, and how much money I had lost.

Estate sale problems

Probably the largest drawback to estate sales is that occasionally you will be unable to find an acceptable estate sale to attend. There may be a lot of estate sales advertised, but none of them sound promising. There will be weeks where there are no acceptable estate sales. Don't compromise your standards for evaluating estate sales; you will usually be disappointed with the sale, and you will be wasting your time. You should also look out for sales that are intentionally made to sound good, but when you get there, the items have been picked over by dealers or by buyers at a pre-sale, or the sale was just embellished to make it sound as if it were going to be a good sale. There is no definite way you can avoid these sales, but don't be surprised if you run into one or two along the way. One other problem you can run into with estate sales is when most of the items are ridiculously overpriced. Again, there is not much you can do in this situation but to leave and chalk it up to experience, or to return at the end of the sale and attempt to negotiate more reasonable prices. Another problem with estate sales is that often there are multiple good sales being conducted at the same time. If I find that there are two great sales, then I try to have my wife or someone else attend one sale while I attend the other.

People at sales also often close doors behind them, stand in the way, move signs, and hide items. You have to be very observant at sales, so that you will not miss anything. I was once at a sale where one of the buyers actually put a "keep out" sign on a door and then closed the door while he searched the room. I wonder to myself how many times this has happened to me before.

Conclusion

I have been going to estate sales for almost twenty years now, and I have never found anything quite as interesting or exciting to do. It has become a hobby, a part-time business, and somewhat of a passion for me. As a hobby, I have put together a number of collections of valuable items—paper advertising, political items, stamps, and other collections. I view these collections as investments that I feel will only appreciate in value over time. As a part-time business, I have made thousands and thousands of dollars buying and selling valuable items. The passion of an estate sale is the excitement of the search and the realization that you could at any time find something extremely valuable. The idea that you could find an object worth $50,000 or $60,000 or even more, something that could make you a lot richer instantly, is very exciting prospect. The passion is the realization that these valuable items are out there, all over the place, just waiting to be discovered. A treasure could be in the back corner of a dark and damp basement, in between some rafters in a dusty attic filled with cobwebs, or right in front of you in the living room of an old Victorian house. Estate sales are treasure hunts for lost treasures. If you have been to an estate sale, then you know what I'm talking about, but if you haven't, then you will only realize the enjoyment and excitement when you go to one.

With this book, I hope to have piqued your interest in estate sales. You will have fun. You will make money—sometimes a lot of money. So get started. Have fun. And good luck!

Glossary of Terms

- **antique co-op or antique mall:** An establishment that rents spaces or booths to dealers where they can sell their items.

- **Bakelite:** A type of plastic usually found in an older item from the forties and fifties. It gives off an acetone smell when rubbed vigorously. Three of the most common colors are bright red, butterscotch, and brown. If you find any items, especially jewelry, made out of a hard plastic in these colors, you should be highly suspicious that it is Bakelite and probably an older item.

- **black light:** Ultraviolet light used to detect the age of some items, especially paper items and glass items. Older glass tends to give off a greenish glow when placed under the light. Newer paper items fluoresce brightly when placed under the light. Any paper items made before about 1960 should not fluoresce under a black light.

- **cast iron:** Usually toys, but also many other items, made from pouring iron into a cast. Very thick and heavy.

- **celluloid:** A plastic ping-pong-like of material used in the twenties and thirties to make many different items, especially small toys, souvenirs, and political pins.

- **cut glass:** An older process in which designs were actually cut into the surface of glass, as opposed to glass items where the design is pressed or molded into the surface. The edges of cut glass are noticeably sharper, and the glass normally fluoresces under black light.

- **crazing:** The minute cracking or pattern of cracking that occurs in the glaze or surface of a ceramic item with aging. It can also be artificially created to make an item appear old.

- **dust cover:** A detachable paper cover, usually very graphic or colorful, used to protect the binding of a book. Most of the time it is very important that a book possess its dust cover; sometimes it is 80 to 90 percent of the value of a book.

- **estate sale:** A sale of person's personal possessions, usually held at the owner's residence. It usually, but not always, includes all the owners' possessions. Furniture, clothes, vehicles, books, etc., are normally all sold at an estate sale.

- **fantasy item:** An item made for the collector market that did not really exist at the time period indicated. Bubblegum cards depicting the *Leave It to Beaver* show did not exist in the fifties when the show was popular, but were made in abundance throughout the eighties and nineties. These types of items have far less value that actual bubblegum cards from the period.

- **foxing:** Brownish discoloration found on older paper items. Sometimes it is artificially added to newer items to make them look old.

- **Lucite:** A clear plastic material used as a substitute for glass in the fifties and sixties to make many items, including purses and kitchen utensils.

- **oxidation:** The change to an item over time when exposed to the atmosphere. It causes most items to lose their luster. If there is no evidence of oxidation, you have to question the age, and therefore the authenticity, of the item.

- **memorabilia:** Any items of the past, concerning different events or matters, that are frequently collected.

- **picture sleeve:** The paper covering on a 45 RPM record. It usually pictures the artist or artists on the record, and it can be 90 percent of the value of the record.

- **pre-sale:** A sale held sometime before the actual estate sale.

- **pressed metal:** A process used to make many items, usually toys, where the toy is made from thick metal pressed over a metal form. It was used in the fifties and earlier.

- **provenance:** The history of an item, its place or source of origin. If you know the provenance of an item, then you can normally determine its authenticity.

- **reserve:** The minimum acceptable bid amount placed on an item up for auction

- **salting:** The process of placing items in an estate sale that are not part of the estate. Often the items are newer and less valuable. It is a form of deception that can be very costly to an incautious buyer.

- **tag sale:** A sale similar to an estate sale, but where most items are tagged with a price. They are usually run by professionals, and prices tend to be somewhat higher than prices at an estate sale.

- **tin litho:** A process where printed graphics are applied directly to tin items. It was commonly used on toys of the forties through the sixties.

- **wear pattern:** This refers to the natural wear to an item from normal use over time, which removes some of the original surface; *e.g.,* the base of any older vase should have noticeable wear to the area that comes in contact with a table.

About the Author

M. Baker is a graduate of University of Pittsburgh who has been actively involved with the antiques and collectible business for over 20 years, especially with its relationship to estate sales.

Made in the USA
Lexington, KY
02 March 2014